Edinburgh
On This Day

Edinburgh
On This Day

Ian Colquhoun

Edinburgh
On This Day

Pitch Publishing Ltd
A2 Yeoman Gate
Yeoman Way
Durrington
BN13 3QZ

Email: info@pitchpublishing.co.uk
Web: www.pitchpublishing.co.uk

First published in the UK by Pitch Publishing, 2014

A CIP catalogue record for this book is available from the British Library.

ISBN: 978-1-909626-66-9
Cover design: Brilliant Orange Creative Services.
Typesetting: Alan Wares.
Editor: Dan Tester www.copymatters.co.uk
Printed in Great Britain. Production managed by Jellyfish Solutions.

DEDICATION

In memory of everyone from Craigshill who was
taken from us too soon.

RIP

ACKNOWLEDGEMENTS

I could not have written this book without the help, support and encouragement kindly provided by the following people.

I would like to thank:

Chris Kelly for pointing me in this direction, John Campbell for doing me a favour, Dan Tester for his patience and understanding, Dorothy and Nigel for letting me pick their brains and borrow their old documents. My uncle Ronnie Merrilees, who seems to know everything about Edinburgh, my family, in particular my mum for supporting me when I had health problems while I was writing it, and the rest of my family for believing in me.

Special thanks to Alastair McBean, the photographer, with additional photography by Kirsty Colquhoun, editorial assistance by Leona King and, of course, Owen Dudley Edwards, for my foreword.

I also owe thanks to the following people for their general support and brilliance:

Tony Divers, Davie McDermott, Jenny Hood, Maggie McDermott, Mark Oakes, John Norton, Leona King, Kirsty Colquhoun, Chris Brown PhD, Stuart MacHardy MA, Sir Tom Farmer, Steve Richards, Alf Tyson, Graham Welham, Brian Warfield, Willy Colquhoun, Bobby Sinnet, Olivia Giles, Lynn Nelson, Janie Peacock, Keith Ferguson, Newington Library, Sandra Dick, Shug and most of the fans on my Facebook page.

FOREWORD

As a historian, it's my job to find out what happened in the past, and to make some kind of sense out of it.

So, it's been very exciting to discover Ian Colquhoun's new kind of history. Many books have been written about Edinburgh and its history – and the city itself acts as its own historian if you know how to contextualise what you see – but Ian has found an exhilaratingly fresh way of enabling us to grasp our past.

Here, Ian uses records and reports of what might often seem minor events in Edinburgh's history to make the city come to life cumulatively. For each day of our own year we find one, two or three snapshots of what made that vivid for the Edinburgh of its time, perhaps for something subsequently completely forgotten, or perhaps for a name or a deed that flashes into our minds whenever we think of the city.

We meet old friends, needing no more than the pleased recognition 'so that was when that happened', balanced by 'I never knew that' on many other dates. And, we find events we cared little about if alive – when it happened – now take on a new life for us.

Ian Colquhoun's Edinburgh is naturally not yours or mine until our absorption in this fascinating book had made it ours. There are other signs of his distinctiveness as a historian, apart from football. Others among us would no doubt notice bad accidents, and their casualties, but he is especially alive to the tragedies of the wounded and maimed. The casual observer may glide over reference to those injured, but not killed, in some local disaster, but this historian knows that injury may be as full a loss as death, in some ways the more so as survival brings new forms of loss. He does not milk these things, but his use of factual accounts brings them a little closer to us than another and more fortunate historian could.

As we walk through the city, touristically, proprietorially, absorbantly we make it and it makes us. But Ian Colquhoun reminds us that our city's history does not unroll itself before our eyes chronologically ...

... in its impact, as though we took Arthur's establishment of his seat as Event 1, or less romantically began with the geological activity more accurately asserting its existence. Our consciousness of the past remakes us, but even as our eyes dart here and there at what the city shows us, different years and decades inextricably mixed up make their impact, and Queen Margaret blends with Queen Mary, and the Scott who brought Waverley to Scotland elides into the Stevenson who left David Balfour outside the British Linen Bank. Our minds have the duty of sorting them out, but our hearts are built up by them one on top of another. So, we will not only understand and enjoy our city more with this book in our hands, we may also find it easier to understand ourselves. God Bless Ian Colquhoun!

Owen Dudley Edwards,
School of History, Classics and Archaeology,
University of Edinburgh
September 2013

INTRODUCTION

Compiling this wee book has been a journey, not least because I have had a number of unrelated problems and setbacks on the way that almost meant I couldn't complete it. The journey has been worth it, though.

Through reading this work, I hope you too will be taken on a journey, as I was: a journey through the past of Scotland's beautiful capital city. Though I grew up in Livingston, part of my family hail from Edinburgh, and through this – and watching football in the city for most of my life – I have loved the place, now my adopted home, all my life.

You'll read about all sorts of events and important decisions that have shaped the city we know and love today. You'll hopefully get some insight into how the city has changed over the centuries, leaving you wanting to read more in-depth books on the subject.

You'll see some problems or customs that we associate solely with modern times have actually been around for decades, if not centuries. You will read about Edinburgh's generosity, its politics, its disasters, its epidemics, its executions and its many battles; both military and social.

From the important decisions that have shaped the city's very appearance and layout, to some of the near farcical cases that have been through its courts. The sporting triumphs and disappointments and, in some cases, the sectarianism in days gone. Thankfully, it is not an issue in the modern era. There are famous events, and some less well-known ones…

Some good decisions that transformed the city. And some 'white elephants' that promised much, but faded into obscurity.

Edinburgh is a city of culture, a city of music, a city of innovation, a city of sport, a city of new beginnings, a city of education and a city of spirituality. It has been a pleasure to research and write about, and I hope the reader enjoys the book as much as I enjoyed writing it. These are some things, large and small, that happened in Edinburgh On This Day…

JANUARY

FRIDAY 1st JANUARY 1779

Edinburgh's ordinary citizens held an unprecedented New Year feast – for the 35 French prisoners of war being held in the castle. The feast included locally grown vegetables and goods from the bakeries in the city, and was permitted by the castle's commander. No such feast was given to prisoners of American or Irish descent, as they were viewed as traitors, not soldiers, and were instead given one pound of bread each with which to 'celebrate' the New Year.

MONDAY 1st JANUARY 1973

Having recently won the cup and having hammered luckless Ayr United 8-0, Hibs travelled to Tynecastle for the New Year Edinburgh Derby. The high-flying Easter Road men were too strong for the Jambos and were 5-0 up by half-time, eventually running out 7-0 winners, with goals from Alex Cropley and a brace apiece by Arthur Duncan, Jimmy O'Rourke and Alan Gordon.

SUNDAY 2nd JANUARY 1949

City firemen were called to a blaze in Duddingston after a suspicious plume of smoke was spotted. There was no blaze, however, as the smoke had been caused by a local resident burning non-standard fuel in his fireplace, much to the disdain of the officers who attended. The first fire in The Lothians of the New Year was not until January 3rd, at a piggery in nearby Broxburn.

THURSDAY 3rd JANUARY 1918

The introduction of maximum pricing for meat caused serious problems at Edinburgh's cattle market. Only 23 bullocks were sold on this day, rather than the usual 800, and many butchers had simply been unable to acquire any stock. Purchasers drew lots to see who would be lucky enough to recieve a bull. One of the biggest meat firms in the city, who usually slaughtered 30 beasts a week, only got one.

TUESDAY 4th JANUARY 1921

Lord Provost Chesser pointed out that spending on the hospital had increased greatly in recent years, but was also quick to praise the dedication of staff and volunteers within the facility, which was still the best funded in Scotland.

SATURDAY 4th JANUARY 1936

Archbishop MacDonald of Edinburgh presented Charles George SSC, of Palmerston Place, with a document from His Holiness the Pope, appointing him a Knight Commander of the Order of St Gregory. One of the most prominent Roman Catholic laymen in Edinburgh, he was an original member of the Catholic Truth Society of Scotland, and for a number of years was treasurer of the Scottish branch of the Society for Propagation of the Faith and the Roman Catholic Society for Foreign Missions.

SATURDAY 5th JANUARY 1946

A 20-year-old man named James Henretty was treated for severe burns and cuts received in an early morning blaze at 11 Wardlaw Place. Only prompt action by the fire brigade prevented the fire spreading to other tenements. Mr Henretty's kitchen and house contents were ruined by the smoke and flames.

TUESDAY 6th JANUARY 1925

The Housing Committee of Edinburgh Town Council, after meeting in the City Chambers, agreed to recommend the Town Council to accept the offer of the Corolito Construction Company to erect 52 houses at Lochend. These revolutionary newly designed houses, which will be erected in blocks of four, will be of three apartments, and will cost from £420 to £440 each. The Corolito Company was formed some time ago to erect houses on the Korrelbelon system, which has been successfully employed in Holland, easing their own housing crisis.

THURSDAY 7th JANUARY 1937

Two Edinburgh boys appeared in court accused of using stolen single shillings to pay for a meal in a Princes Street café. Investigations had revealed the boys had stolen the coins after breaking into a house on Calder Medway and opening the gas and electricity meters. The boys pleaded guilty and were each placed on probation for a year.

SUNDAY 8th JANUARY 1729

After hearing reports from concerned citizens, the Town Guard arrested two women in Edinburgh for the crime of wearing men's clothing. The two unnamed ladies vehemently protested their innocence but were still led away.

FRIDAY 9th JANUARY 1970

Edinburgh Police Traffic Department today warned that a shortage of lollipop men and adverse weather conditions could lead to many children having accidents during the cold snap. Eighteen lollipop men were off sick and six vacancies were still to be filled.

FRIDAY 10th JANUARY 1919

The Plans and Works Committee of Edinburgh Town Council met today and agreed to approach the North British Railway Company with a view to coming to an arrangement where the clock on the North British Station Hotel may be lit up at night for the benefit – and health and safety – of the city's citizens.

TUESDAY 11th JANUARY 1983

Edinburgh's 29 public toilets were to be given a facelift, and an additional seven public conveniences to be built, as part of a scheme costing over one million pounds. The cost was to be partially covered by an increase in usage fees from two pence to five pence.

FRIDAY 12th JANUARY 1912

Charles Weir, aged 18 and from Abbeyhill, was discovered wandering Arthur's Seat with an old fashioned rifle, shooting rabbits. Mr Weir had a gunshot wound to his left breast which he claimed to have received when his rifle went off as he was scrambling up rocks. A shepherd who initially assisted Mr Weir noted that the man's single-shot rifle was still loaded, indicating that he had reloaded his gun AFTER wounding himself. A report was sent to the police.

SATURDAY 13th JANUARY 1968

Bernard Miller, chairman of the John Lewis Partnership, announced plans for a new £3m five-storey department store at St James Square, which would create around 780 new jobs. The building was expected to open in time for Christmas 1971.

SUNDAY 14th JANUARY 1872

After keeping watch over his old master's grave for over 14 years, the Terrier dog Greyfriars Bobby finally passed away. He has since become famous, being commemorated in book, film and statue.

FACING EASTWARD ALONG PRINCES STREET FROM THE TOP DECK OF AN EDINBURGH BUS

WEDNESDAY 15th JANUARY 1941

A sentence of 60 days' imprisonment was passed by Sheriff Jamieson at Edinburgh Sheriff Court on John McIntyre Hill. He admitted having obtained board and lodgings to the value of £21 in an Edinburgh hotel without paying, or intending to pay. It was stated that the accused had stayed at the hotel over 12 months earlier and had left without paying his bill. He was arrested in the Army, and when he had previously stood before the court he had stated he would pay the bill as he had fallen heir to an inheritance. Sentence was then deferred but the bill had not been paid. The accused said his inheritance had not yet been received. Sheriff Jamieson did not approve of the court being made a place for the recovery of debt. The accused had swindled a hotelkeeper and seven months had elapsed since he had failed to adhere to his original promise to pay.

SUNDAY 16th JANUARY 1707

The mentally disturbed Earl of Drumlanrig was locked up in Queensferry House in the Canongate while his father negotiated the Treaty of Union in Edinburgh. Hunger took the Earl, and he soon escaped his room in search of food. All he could find was a kitchen boy, so he cooked him on a spit and ate him. He had eaten most of his victim before the horrified staff uncovered his crime.

SATURDAY 17th JANUARY 1795

Duddingston Curling Society became formally organised, one of the first in the country, after playing 'unofficially' for a number of years on Duddingston Loch when it was frozen during winter.

MONDAY 18th JANUARY 1937

A report that the Government had placed an order for nearly five million gas masks with the North British Rubber Company in Edinburgh, was investigated by a representative of *The Scotsman* newspaper. At the offices of the company it was stated that while the firm had received orders from the Government for the manufacture of gas masks, none of these amounted to anything like the figure mentioned. As it turned out, the Nazis never resorted to dropping gas anyway.

FRIDAY 19th JANUARY 2007

A century of care finally drew to a close as the old Eastern General Hospital at Seafield finally closed its doors for the last time. In its heyday, the Eastern General Hospital was a central pillar of the Leith community, and its closure after 100 years marked the end of an era. Though most services provided by the hospital had been moved to other units gradually over the years, it had remained a non-emergency hospital, one of the last services to leave the building being the SMART prosthetic limbs clinic. The facility was to be relocated to the Astley Ainslie Hospital on the city's Southside.

FRIDAY 20th JANUARY 1950

Following the recent meeting of Leith Dock Commission (LDC), at which proposals were discussed for a scheduled flying-boat service to operate between Leith and Falmouth, further discussions took place on this day with the Ministry of Civil Aviation. The Ministry were approached with a view to obtaining sanction for the use of Leith waters as an airport. At the last LDC meeting it was stated a letter had been received from Christian Salvesen on behalf of Aquila Airways who had been approached by a Falmouth company to charter flying-boats for a scheduled service between Leith and Falmouth, and enquiring into the possibility of Leith being licensed as a civil airport. Whether the project would be viable remained to be seen.

TUESDAY 21st JANUARY 1930

In a resounding display of anti-war sentiment, Edinburgh Trades and Labour Council, at their meeting, passed a resolution assuring the Prime Minister of their cordial support in the efforts he had made towards international peace. They also asked him to urge upon the Naval Disarmament Conference, sitting in London, that such a programme would – at least – accomplish the abolition of all capital ships and submarines and the drastic limitation of cruisers and other vessels of war. The resolution had been forwarded to the council by the No More War Movement. After the discussion, the secretary was instructed to write to headquarters in London and make a request for speakers who would not be so familiar to an Edinburgh audience, and would therefore be likely to draw a larger crowd.

MONDAY 22nd JANUARY 1934

An outbreak of 'joyriding' was the talk of the town. Five motor cars were stolen on Sunday night from various districts, and afterwards found abandoned in the streets. Among the stolen cars was one which was driven by the daughter of Lord Provost Thomson, and which, at the time of the theft, was standing in Moray Place. This car was afterwards retrieved in India Street. The other points from which cars were taken were in Rothesay Terrace, York Place, Hope Street, and Chalmers Crescent. All the offences occurred between 7pm and 10pm and the cars were recovered by the police within a short period of their being stolen. Two men who were arrested on the previous Saturday night were in custody, charged with intent to steal cars from Brunswick Street, while on this day, a sentence of two months' imprisonment was passed in Edinburgh Sheriff Court on William Steedman, a motor mechanic, who admitted having stolen a motor car.

WEDNESDAY 23rd JANUARY 1946

An experienced railway worker was killed in a tragic accident. Engaged on lookout duty in connection with the clearing of points near Waverley Station, Joseph James Brown (47), an LNER worker in Edinburgh, was struck by an engine and killed instantly. Tracks had to be closed while the tragic mess was cleared.

SATURDAY 24th JANUARY 1948

Hibs manager Willie McCartney collapsed and died in Coatbridge during Hibs' Scottish Cup match against Albion Rovers at Cliftonhill. Despite his tragic death, Hibs became only the second team outside the Old Firm since 1904 to win the Scottish League championship when they lifted the title three months later.

TUESDAY 25th JANUARY 1927

William Glendinning, a milkman from Bread Street, died while making a valiant attempt to stop his horse from bolting. Mr Glendinning was standing on his lorry in a yard on Restalrig Road when the horse became frightened and tried to run away. The milkman jumped off his lorry and tried to grab the horse's reins, but in doing so was jammed between a gatepost and his lorry. He was pronounced dead upon arrival at The Royal Infirmary.

FRIDAY 26th JANUARY 1861

The One O'Clock gun was fired for the first time from Edinburgh Castle's half-moon battery. It fired a blank 18-pound shell. The shell was fired towards Inchkeith Island out in the Firth of Forth.

MONDAY 27th JANUARY 1936

Archibald Smith, a labourer, who resided at 9 Hawkhill Avenue, Edinburgh, met with a shocking death on this day. He was engaged in placing a new water tank in position at the rear of a drying room in laundry premises in Causewayside, when his clothing got caught in a revolving shaft. He was smashed against the wall and fatally injured.

WEDNESDAY 28th JANUARY 1829

William Burke, one of two men caught murdering people and stealing dead bodies in Edinburgh with the purpose of selling the cadavers to anatomist Robert Knox, was hanged in the city. His accomplice, William Hare, escaped the death penalty by turning King's Evidence against Burke. In total, the pair had murdered at least 17 innocent people. Most of the bodies fetched around £7.

FRIDAY 29th JANUARY 1904

In front of Sheriff Henderson, in Edinburgh Summary Court today, Robert Caddeo and Robert Dodds, two taxi-drivers, denied a charge of having assaulted Robert Robertson, Dysart, by compressing his throat, pulling and dragging him about, beating him with their fists, and a whip. They were also charged with having stolen twelve shillings from Robertson and having driven their cab over him, thus rendering him unconscious. Both the cab drivers were given 40 days in prison.

TUESDAY 30th JANUARY 1945

A detachment of the National Fire Service had to be called to Portobello Baths to pump water out of the basement. The reason for the flooding was not yet ascertained, but it was thought it may, in part, be due to the recent damage to the promenade by heavy seas in the Firth of Forth. The flooding in no way interfered with the use of the popular swimming baths.

THURSDAY 31st JANUARY 1918

'The Battle of May Island' occurred in the Firth of Forth. One hundred and three officers and sailors died when two flotillas of submarines and cruisers collided with minesweeping vessels which were at work in the area and unaware of the presence of their comrades.

FEBRUARY

FRIDAY 1st FEBRUARY 1929

The number of influenza patients in Edinburgh was on the increase. In both business firms and schools there were many absentees due to the epidemic. An inquiry at the Electricity Department of Edinburgh Corporation learned that, although a week ago, conditions were normal, there was a much higher percentage of people off work as a result of the flu.

THURSDAY 2nd FEBRUARY 1989

British Coal warned all Scottish pits would be forced to close almost immediately if the SSEB proceeded with their plans to stop buying their coal after March 31st. The current deal expired at the end of March, and looked unlikely to be renewed, despite increased productivity and output rates at Scottish pits.

FRIDAY 3rd FEBRUARY 1922

No further outbreaks of foot-and-mouth disease were reported in the capital, with all infected carcasses expected to have been buried by the end of the day. The market was not expected to open again for at least another week while cleaning was in progress, and all hunts in the area had been discontinued for the time being. Livestock traffic into the city was being closely monitored.

WEDNESDAY 4th FEBRUARY 1818

'The Honours of Scotland' also known as the Crown and Regalia of Scotland, consisting of the Crown, the Sceptre and the Sword of State, were finally put on display in Edinburgh Castle after being hidden for over 100 years following the Treaty of Union. Sir Walter Scott was responsible for their rediscovery. The items had been hidden so they could not be used as rallying symbols by Jacobites/Nationalists.

MONDAY 5th FEBRUARY 1979

Edinburgh's residents were warned to take care when visiting Cramond Island after four shivering schoolboys were rescued from the icy waters. The boys, who were all local, were pulled out of the water by the South Queensferry Inshore Lifeboat after their desperate cries for help were heard by passers-by on Cramond foreshore.

THURSDAY 6th FEBRUARY 1969

Havoc hit Edinburgh's public transport system, with over 100 buses off the road due to crews not turning up for work. A Corporation spokesman blamed the fiasco on staff sickness and staff not turning up to do overtime as requested. The situation, which had worsened since schoolchildren came back from their holidays, was expected to ease during the day, but to worsen once more during the evening rush-hour.

TUESDAY 7th FEBRUARY 1989

Edinburgh celebrated a great and prestigious economic boost with the announcement of a new genetic research centre for Edinburgh University that could bring in over £15 million worth of investment over the next ten years. The centre will be based in the King's Buildings on West Mains Road. University Principal Sir David Smith said the announcement was "good news for the university and good news for Edinburgh".

FRIDAY 8th FEBRUARY 1946

A beat patrol car, a new Edinburgh police idea for 'covering' the suburban and outer areas, is operating in the capital. In touch with headquarters by wireless, the car has a roving commission and the crew is there to help out the constables on the long and lonely beats. The vehicle is also in contact with the regular road traffic patrols and can be at any spot within a few minutes. Chief Constable Morren pointed out the innovation is proving so successful that he hoped to expand the scheme in the future.

THURSDAY 9th FEBRUARY 1989

Archaeologists in Edinburgh discovered the remains of a 16th-century house some six feet below the Royal Mile. The building, the Abbot's Town House, was the lodgings of the Abbots of Melrose.

MONDAY 10th FEBRUARY 1567

The body of Lord Darnley, husband of Mary Queen of Scots and cousin of Queen Elizabeth of England, was found in the orchard at Kirk O'Field near the Royal Mile, alongside that of his valet. He was found wearing only his night shirt. A great explosion had rocked the building during the night and Darnley was strangled to death when he rushed outside to escape the house. Queen Mary was later accused of being in on the plot to murder him.

SUNDAY 11th FEBRUARY 1945

Burglars who broke into the premises of Karter and Co. furriers, 72 George Street, Edinburgh, got away with a haul of furs and fur coats valued at between £2,000 and £3,000. It was believed the burglary took place between 1am and 3am, as the premises were in order when examined by a policeman on the beat at 1am. Entrance was gained by breaking the gate and forcing the lock on the main door. The furs taken away included musquash, baby seal and other types, and were in the form of coats, capes, wraps, ties and other articles. Police were anxious to hear from any person who may have seen a vehicle or persons in suspicious circumstances in the vicinity of the shop during the night or early morning.

THURSDAY 12th FEBRUARY 1953

A postbox marked 'EIIR' – The Queen's English title – was blown up at The Inch by unknown persons who objected to the inscription on it as there has only ever been one Queen Elizabeth in Scotland. Previous attempts to destroy the postbox with gelignite and with a 7lb hammer had ended in failure. The box was soon replaced by one bearing the correct cipher.

SATURDAY 13th FEBRUARY 1915

The Edinburgh Tram Company announced its intention to employ female conductors, having received some 60 applications from women. The company intended to deploy the new workers on The Mound and North-Side routes where fares were easier to calculate and there were fewer big crowds to handle.

FRIDAY 14th FEBRUARY 2003

Celebrity sheep Dolly, of the Roslin Institute in Edinburgh, died. Almost seven years old, the latter part of her short but interesting life was plagued by arthritis and other health conditions, which many suspected were caused by her not being naturally created. In the end she was put to sleep to ease her pain. Dolly produced six lambs during her relatively short life. Her stuffed remains are now displayed at Edinburgh's National Museum of Scotland.

CITY SKYLINE FROM OCEAN TERMINAL VIEWPOINT

TUESDAY 15th FEBRUARY 1944

A demonstration of mass miniature radiography was given at the Royal Infirmary of Edinburgh, for the benefit of doctors and other interested parties. It was by arrangement with the managers that General Radiological Ltd gave the demonstration, using a 'Kokak' fluorographic unit in conjunction with a four-valve X-ray set, and the proceedings were opened by Lieut-Colonel AD Stewart, superintendent of the Infirmary. The audience was shown how any existing X-ray sets of suitable output could be used for mass miniature radiography by the addition of a readily available camera unit. The working and adjustment of the apparatus was explained, and in the course of the afternoon six patients were seen being X-rayed. An opportunity of examining the films themselves through a magnifying glass was also given to those in attendance.

MONDAY 16th FEBRUARY 1941

The 'Railings for Scrap – Scrap for Victory' campaign was gaining impetus in Edinburgh. Since last Monday, when Lord Provost Henry Steele, in opening the railings exhibition in North Bridge, announced he was giving the railings around his house for war material, some 23 other house owners followed his example. A further 19 owners were awaiting the consent of superiors. It was expected sufficient iron and steel would be obtained from these 24 houses, including the Lord Provost's, to make three 3.7" anti-aircraft guns. The indications were that many other houseowners were considering the donation of their railings. The Cleansing Department appealed for a thousand house owners to follow the patriotic gesture of the Lord Provost.

SATURDAY 17th FEBRUARY 1968

A thrilling Scottish Cup tie at Tannadice saw Hearts edge out Dundee Utd 6-5, the Jambos being inspired by Scandinavian player Rene Moller. Nine thousand fans saw the match.

TUESDAY 18th FEBRUARY 1947

Outbreaks of foot-and-mouth disease were confirmed at Gorgie (Edinburgh) and in nearby Broxburn. In both cases the animals affected were pigs. A standstill order covering areas of 15 miles radius round both centres was immediately put into operation. One result of this was no livestock sales in Edinburgh on this day. The standstill order was due to last for about two weeks, or until further news from the Ministry of Agriculture's Divisional Veterinary Officer.

THURSDAY 19th FEBRUARY 1959

The question of whether or not women had justified the granting of the voting franchise was raised at the City Chambers. Members of the Parliamentary Branch of the Edinburgh Women Citizens Association were so impressed with the arguments led by the two principal speakers that they waived their right to vote on the subject. Miss Isobel L Sinclair, advocate, Edinburgh, offered £20 if any member present could produce evidence of a group of men similarly gathered together to prove that men had justified the vote.

SUNDAY 20th FEBRUARY 1994

Easter Road was the venue for an all-Edinburgh Scottish Cup fourth-round tie between Hibs and Hearts, shown live on TV throughout the UK. Hibs, who had been struggling in this fixture and had looked jaded since losing the cup final to Rangers the previous October, were looking to end a winless run against Hearts that had lasted since early 1989. John Robertson gave Hearts an early lead, before Keith Wright equalised for Hibs just before the interval. Hearts' backs were against the wall for most of the second half, then, with only four minutes remaining, and with the match heading for a midweek replay at Tynecastle, a dreadful error in judgement by Hibs defender Dave Beaumont allowed Hearts substitute Wayne Foster an unimpeded run at goal from which he scored, much to the jubilation of the away fans. Foster had hitherto been a figure of ridicule to fans of both clubs, but this goal sealed his place in Edinburgh football folklore. The fixture was marred by sporadic outbreaks of violence throughout the city centre in the aftermath, though there were few arrests.

MONDAY 21st FEBRUARY 1842

The first inter-city railway line between Glasgow on the west coast, and Edinburgh on the east, made its inaugural journey. It was opened by none other than Queen Victoria herself.

TUESDAY 21st FEBRUARY 1995

Scotland's fringe players got their chance in a B international against Northern Ireland at Easter Road. A freezing but boisterous 'home' support saw Scotland thump the Irishmen 3-0 with goals from Stephen Wright, and one apiece from Hibs players Darren Jackson and Steven Tweed. The latter two's goals triggered an impromptu chorus of 'Hibees' from the East Terrace, despite the match being an international.

TUESDAY 22nd FEBRUARY 2005

Residents of Edinburgh voted against the introduction of congestion charging in the city by a margin of approximately three to one. Around 290,000 residents were asked if they were in favour of cordons, similar to those in London, and under consideration in Bristol. More than 74% of the voters rejected the council's plan. The turnout for the postal ballot was 61.8%. There were 133,678 votes against and 45,965 in favour. Leader of Edinburgh City Council, Labour councillor Donald Anderson, said; "The idea is now dead and buried for Edinburgh but we are as committed as ever to further improving our city's transport."

SATURDAY 23rd FEBRUARY 1303

The Battle of Roslin, in which a Scots army of 8,000, led by Sir Simon Fraser, Sinclair of Rosslyn and the Red Comyn, surprised an English army of 30,000 (English numbers exaggerated as usual) led by Sir John Seagrave, and defeated them in a rare Scottish victory over their traditional enemy.

THURSDAY 23rd FEBRUARY 1928

'The Edinburgh Stonehenge' was the subject of a lantern lecture delivered by Professor V Gordon Childe, Edinburgh University, to the members of the Greater Edinburgh Club in the Synod Hall. Professor Childs explained this was a stone circle between Lochend and Newbridge, close to the Glasgow road.

SATURDAY 24th FEBRUARY 1923

Steam train the 'Flying Scotsman' went into service with London and North Eastern Railway (LNER), on the London (King's Cross) to Edinburgh route. It would eventually go on to 'clock up' over two million journey miles.

SATURDAY 24th FEBRUARY 2001

Hearts scored seven goals for the first time in over 15 years by beating Dunfermline 7-1 at Tynecastle, Andy Kirk and Colin Cameron among the goal scorers. Jason Dair netted a late consolation for the Pars before Robert Tomaschek completed the rout in the 67th minute. Dunfermline had previously lost only one of their last 11 games, against Rangers.

FRIDAY 25th FEBRUARY 1938

Among the warrants granted by Edinburgh Dean of Guild Court, at a sitting in the City Chambers, was one to Edinburgh Corporation for 148 dwelling houses at Crewe Road North. This was the first development of the West Pilton area, where there was a provisional layout for over 2,000 houses. Of the 148, two were of five apartments, 107 of four apartments and 39 of three apartments. The architect was Mr E J MacRae, the city architect. The petition of the Murrayfield Ice Rink and Sports Stadium to erect a sports stadium at the Scottish Rugby Union ground was called, and the record was declared closed. A date would be fixed by the court when the parties would be heard in their pleadings.

SATURDAY 25th FEBRUARY 1989

The Scotsman reported taxi fares in Edinburgh could rise by up to 27 per cent this year – their biggest single increase. The public would have a chance to make their views known before the jump was agreed. City councillors have accepted increased tariff plans from the recently formed Edinburgh Licensed Taxi Association and the proposals would now be advertised.

SATURDAY 26th FEBRUARY 1939

During its 11 days, nearly 179,000 people attended the Royal Air Force Aircraft and National Services Exhibition in the Waverley Market, Edinburgh.

MONDAY 26th FEBRUARY 1979

Roderick Marshall from Edinburgh had the best brain in Britain – and that's official. He won the title of Superbrain 1979 in a national competition organised by MENSA and admitted it has caused him some embarrassment. Roderick, 22, of 13 Drumbrae Walk, won the local regional heat of the competition which was run through the *Evening News* before he went on to the finals in Birmingham.

TUESDAY 27th FEBRUARY 1560

The second Treaty of Berwick between England and Scotland was signed, providing English assistance to remove the French forces of Mary of Guise, who still occupied Leith Fort and Inchkeith Island in the Firth of Forth. An English army and navy were sent to help the Scots end Mary's regency so that Scotland would be free to have its religious reformation.

SATURDAY 27th FEBRUARY 1864

British Prime Minister Lord Palmerston condemned the Water of Leith as a 'nuisance that is in a worse state than the Thames', in reference to the raw sewage and rubbish contained in it. City officials, including the Lord Provost, had initially been too embarrassed to let the Prime Minister visit the notoriously filthy waterway.

SUNDAY 28th FEBRUARY 1638

The second National Covenant was signed in Greyfriars Churchyard, Edinburgh. Its signatories, noble and commoner alike, were rejecting the proposed religious reforms of King Charles I and his attempts to force religious uniformity upon his three kingdoms. The first covenant had been drafted in 1581.

MONDAY 28th FEBRUARY 1949

Edinburgh Corporation protested to the South East Scotland Electricity Consultative Council against the increase in the domestic electricity tariff, and urged a substantial reduction should be made in the running charge and that the additional one for the winter period should be refunded to customers. The protest was in the form of a statement prepared by Treasurer Miller, and was presented to a meeting of the council.

MONDAY 29th FEBRUARY 1932

The measles epidemic has spread still further in Edinburgh and last week 627 cases were notified while three deaths occurred. An official of the Public Health Department of Edinburgh Corporation today told a representative of *The Scotsman* that it was impossible to say whether the height of the epidemic had been reached or not. The number of cases notified last week was - he pointed out - somewhat similar to that reached about two years ago, when a fairly bad epidemic of measles was prevalent in Edinburgh. It was said that measles epidemics recurred every two years. He did not think the outbreak would be so severe as the previous one because there had been so many cases during the epidemic of two years ago that there should not now be many susceptible children in the city. So far, he added, the present epidemic had not been of a particularly bad type. There were 125 cases reported during the epidemic's first week, and that had risen to 627 by its fifth.

MARCH

FRIDAY 1st MARCH 1675

James Mitchell was executed by drowning in the Nor Loch. It had been decided to do the deed at 4am so the public would not have to set eyes on this notorious man, who had been found guilty of homosexuality and sodomy.

FRIDAY 1st MARCH 1940

Fire broke out at a house at 10 West End Place, Dalry Road, Edinburgh, early this afternoon, destroying the furniture and contents of two rooms and a lobby on the top floor and 30 feet of roofing. The flames were extinguished by an engine from the Angle Park Station. Members of the AFS assisted the regular firemen in tackling the blaze.

THURSDAY 2nd MARCH 1911

The War Office invited tenders for work in connection with the proposed cavalry depot at nearby Dunbar. The erection of a new barrack block for four non-commissioned officers and 160 men, and one block of troop stables at Castle Park Barracks, was proposed. Tenders were to be delivered 'not later than Wednesday 22nd'. Following the decision of the War Office, which was published in August of last year, to place the cavalry depot for Scotland at Dunbar instead of at Piershill Barracks, Edinburgh, Mr Haldane sent a letter to Lord Provost Brown, in which he indicated the decision did not affect the prospect of a cavalry regiment coming to Edinburgh as soon as the barracks being built at Redford were completed.

FRIDAY 2nd MARCH 1923

The sum of £17 was raised by the pupils of Castle Hill School, Edinburgh, at a concert in aid of the Police-Aided Boot Fund. The entertainment included a dancing exhibition, and special items by the infants. Mr Sterling Craig, member of the Education Authority and Councillor Gorman, congratulated the teachers and pupils on the success of the concert. Councillor Watt, convener of the Police Fund, also spoke and thanked them for their efforts.

WEDNESDAY 3rd MARCH 1847

Alexander Graham Bell – whose most famous invention was none other than the humble telephone – was born in Edinburgh.

TUESDAY 3rd MARCH 1925

News reached Edinburgh of the scaling of Mount Aconcagua, the highest peak in the Andes, by a local man and Mr Mervyn Frederick Ryan, CBE, an Englishman who held the post of the chief mechanical engineer to the Central Argentine Railway. This was Mr Ryan's third attempt at reaching the summit of Aconcagua, and, as on the two previous occasions, he was accompanied on his expedition by Mr James Cochrane, a native of Edinburgh, who was educated at Daniel Stewart's College and Edinburgh University. Cochrane and Ryan's feat was a notable one, the summit having only been reached by two other climbers.

FRIDAY 3rd MARCH 1950

Mr Alastair Simm, the Scottish actor and Lord Rector of Edinburgh University, signed the Scottish Covenant. He was visited the previous evening at the King's Theatre, Edinburgh, before his performance in James Bridie's new play *Mr Gillie*, by Nigel Tranter, chairman of the Edinburgh area of the Covenant Committee, to whom he gave the following message: "I find myself in complete agreement with all the aims of the Scottish Covenant. I have always disliked that narrow and false nationalism which is the greatest obstacle to ultimate world government, as opposed to this truer love of country which is very properly 'houseproud' and hates dependency on any but its own kin and kind. With the Covenant envisaging this latter altruistic and objective form of nationalism, then, of course, I am delighted to sign."

FRIDAY 4th MARCH 1457

In an attempt to ensure Scotland had an abundance of trained men to call up in the event of war or civil unrest, King James II decreed in an Act of Parliament at Edinburgh, that there should be regular target practice and military parades and that 'football and golf be utterly cried down and not used'. This was the first time that the games had been mentioned in Scottish documents.

TUESDAY 4th MARCH 1890

The Forth Rail Bridge, spanning the Firth of Forth, was officially opened by HRH The Prince of Wales, who paid tribute to the many workers who had died during its construction.

TUESDAY 5th MARCH 1929

Roller-skating en masse returned to Edinburgh at the Marine Gardens Ballroom in Portobello. A very diverse crowd of over 1,000 skaters meandered around the spacious illuminated dancehall, and a section of the floor was set aside for skating novices to find their feet. Music was supplied by a Marconiphone, which cost some £800 to install.

TUESDAY 5th MARCH 1985

Tory councillors in Edinburgh raged as a red flag was hoisted above the City Chambers to mark the first time the city had approved a socialist budget. Labour group secretary Jimmy Burnett defended the gesture as it marked a 'historic occasion', while Tory spokesman Paul Martin called the flag 'utterly irresponsible' and warned it would ruin the city's tourist industry as visitors to the city might associate the flag with full-blown communism and be deterred from visiting again in the future.

WEDNESDAY 6th MARCH AD608

St Balfred, the reclusive hermit monk who lived on the Bass Rock just off North Berwick, died from an unknown disease. The island would later become a bird sanctuary.

SATURDAY 7th MARCH 1744

The Honourable Company of Edinburgh Golfers was founded. The oldest golf club in the world, it produced thirteen 'Rules of Golf' for its first competition, which was played for the 'Silver Club'. The first winner of the trophy only just escaped beheading for becoming Bonnie Prince Charlie's personal surgeon during the Jacobite Uprising the following year. The club played on the five holes at Leith Links for nearly a century.

MONDAY 8th MARCH 1948

James Wolstenholme (38), a window cleaner, who resided at West Fountain Place in Edinburgh, fell a distance of 60 feet when cleaning a window on the top flat of a tenement in Ardmillan Terrace. He received severe head injuries, from which he died about 40 minutes later in the Royal Infirmary, despite the valiant efforts of doctors and his rescuers.

SATURDAY 9th MARCH 1566

Scots nobles burst into the bed chamber of Queen Mary at Holyrood and murdered her advisor David Rizzio by stabbing him to death. The nobles had grown suspicious of the little Italian and jealous of his influence over the Queen. One of the murderers even pointed a loaded pistol at the Queen's heavily pregnant stomach during the attack. The Queen would later milk this incident for propaganda purposes. Scots nobles had suspected, wrongly, that Queen Mary and Rizzio were lovers.

TUESDAY 9th MARCH 1948

The Ministry of Works expressed hope that from April onwards the public would be able to hire rowing boats at St Margaret's Loch, Holyrood Park, Edinburgh. Hiring had ceased about four years previously when boating was made impossible after large bulks of timber for repairing railway bridges were dumped in the loch as a wartime measure. The wood was removed some time later, but an invitation to boat hirers to send in tenders for the letting of boats on the loch brought no immediate response. On this day, the Ministry invited tenders for a five-year contract and hoped for better success in the coming year.

THURSDAY 10th MARCH 1927

An extraordinary case of sheep-worrying within the boundaries of the capital occurred in the King's Park, Edinburgh, early this morning, when about 30 sheep were killed or fatally injured on the slopes and crags of Arthur's Seat. The police were inclined to take a serious view of the matter, and a watch was set in the area. The sheep involved in the affair were from a flock of 400 belonging to Mr Robert Nichol, which had been grazing in the neighbourhood of Dunsapie Loch. A shepherd, going up the hillside at nine o'clock in the morning, found two dogs – stated to be an Airedale and a mongrel Collie – chasing the sheep. The shepherd made attempts, assisted by a boy, to drive the dogs off and they eventually succeeded. But, by the time the dogs had been driven off, a great amount of damage had been done to the flock. Many sheep had been driven up on to the higher slopes and had fled, frightened and uncontrolled, over rocks and crags.

MONDAY 11th MARCH 1929

An order removing three children from the custody of their mother Rosalind Cuthbert, or Lindsay, of 16a Begg's Buildings, Edinburgh, on account of 'unsatisfactory surroundings' was made by Sheriff Orr at Edinburgh Sheriff Court. The petition for the removal of the children, which was presented by Mr George Shirran, chief inspector of the National Society for the Prevention of Cruelty to Children, asked that the eldest of the children, a boy, aged eight, and a girl, aged six, be sent to industrial schools, and the third child, a boy of three, be taken care of by the Society, for such period as the Court saw fit.

FRIDAY 11th MARCH 1938

Plans for a new primary school were passed at a sitting of the Edinburgh Dean of Guild Court held in the City Chambers, Lord Dean of Guild Finlayson presiding. The school, which included a janitor's house and play sheds, was to be built in Sighthill Loan, at a cost estimated at £45,000. There would be accommodation for 1,050 pupils. Built of artificial stone and brick roughcast, the building was two storeys high, containing 21 classrooms and two halls.

FRIDAY 12th MARCH 1937

After a blizzard that had continued with occasional clear intervals for about 24 hours, Edinburgh lay under one of the heaviest falls of snow the city had experienced for years. Transport services were disorganised, and a number of accidents to pedestrians, who had fallen on slippery streets, were reported. Although much less severe than they became later, outdoor conditions were wintry enough during the morning and afternoon. Driven by a north-easterly wind, the snow covered Edinburgh in white and made the streets picturesque where there was no traffic, and very uncomfortable underfoot where the snow had been churned into slush. Several townsfolk were injured by the blizzard and taken to hospital.

FRIDAY 12th MARCH 1972

The Bells Mills in Dean Village were destroyed in a ferocious explosion. Though there were no fatalities, several workers were injured, one so badly he was never able to work again.

HIBS FANS CELEBRATE THEIR 2007 CUP WIN AT HAMPDEN

FRIDAY 13th MARCH 1935

Workmen engaged in draining excavations on the north side of the Castle Park Barracks parade ground at nearby Dunbar unearthed several skulls and bones. Some years before, scores of skulls, and other parts of skeletons, were discovered in another part of the park. The remains were believed to be those of combatants who engaged in countless conflicts for the capture of Dunbar Castle hundreds of years ago. Their wonderful state of preservation was stated to be due to the dry and sandy nature of the soil.

THURSDAY 13th MARCH 1941

After nearly six months' respite, the Luftwaffe returned to Edinburgh with a vengeance, dropping over 100 incendiary bombs on the city's Abbeyhill area following an earlier raid on Clydeside.

THURSDAY 14th MARCH 1314

Sir Thomas Randolph captured Edinburgh Castle from the English after a night escalade – made possible by information from a local man named William Francis – who led a hand-picked team of Scottish men-at-arms up a discrete path, allowing them to surprise and overwhelm the garrison. The castle's defences were then destroyed, preventing them from being used by the English in future.

MONDAY 14th MARCH 1689

A sizeable majority of the Scottish Parliament voted to support the accession to the throne of William of Orange and Mary Stuart, after Mary's father, King James the VII and II, had been forced off the English throne following a palace coup in November 1688. Edinburgh's common folk responded by going on a drinking binge that degenerated into rioting. The 'revolution' was by no means accepted by all. James Graham of Claverhouse, Viscount Dundee, earlier left Edinburgh in disgust at Parliament's decision to abandon the Catholic King James in favour of the new regime, heading north in the company of 60 soldiers vowing to raise an army for James, and leaving the Duke of Gordon in command of Edinburgh Castle with its garrison of barely 80 soldiers. They were also loyal to King James, and would face the wrath of the new regime. A siege loomed.

FRIDAY 14th MARCH 1823

Brothel-keeper Mary McKinnon was hanged in Edinburgh in front of over 20,000 spectators. She had thrown a knife at drunk men who had refused to leave her establishment, accidentally killing one of them.

WEDNESDAY 15th MARCH 1933

One thousand motorists, in 357 cars, faced their second night without sleep in the 1,000 mile RAC rally which concluded at Hastings the next day. At Edinburgh – the halfway house of the rally – no serious mishaps were reported. The driver of a sports car lost a tyre when he was travelling at speed but, although the vehicle skidded and crashed into a bank, it was practically undamaged. Cars to the number of 174, which were participating in the RAC rally, reached Edinburgh and were directed by signs attached to lamp posts. The drivers were due to check in at the Edinburgh control room in the North British Station Hotel.

THURSDAY 16th MARCH 1905

A public meeting, called by the Lord Provost in response to a petition signed by 1,200 persons, was held in the Freemasons' Hall, Edinburgh, to consider the holding of a Scottish National Exhibition in the city in 1907. The requisition stated a movement had been made to promote an exhibition of arts, science, industries, inventions, literature, produce, and manufacturing, and that it had been resolved by the subscribers to give it their full support. The petitioners suggested public bodies throughout the country should be invited as soon as possible to co-operate and assist in the movement, and mentioned a most desirable site, which was readily accessible by railway and car systems, was already available at Murrayfield.

THURSDAY 17th MARCH 1328

The Treaty of Edinburgh between King Robert I and England's Edward I, which recognised Scotland's independence, was signed, ending the protracted 32-year War of Independence.

SATURDAY 17th MARCH 1984

Scotland won Rugby's Grand Slam at Murrayfield – for the first time in 59 years – by beating France 21-12.

FRIDAY 18th MARCH 1689

David Leslie, the pro-English Earl of Leven, raised a regiment of 800 men in the space of only a few hours with the intention of defending the capital from Jacobite supporters of King James VII. A volley from the regiment later killed the Scottish Jacobites' leader, John Graham of Claverhouse ('Bonnie Dundee') at the Battle of Killiecrankie, just as the Jacobites had completed a famous, yet ultimately Pyrrhic victory. The regiment was one of only two government battalions not to flee the field in terror that day, and was henceforth allowed to recruit in Edinburgh without the permission of the Lord Provost – a significant honour. They later fought on the government side at Culloden in 1746 as 'Sempill's' and then became known as the King's Own Scottish Borderers.

THURSDAY 18th MARCH 1751

Two nurses, Jean Waldie and Helen Torrance, were executed for body-snatching and murder in Edinburgh. After they had been conned by local students into handing over a body in their charge for nothing, the pair were eventually caught and charged when they tried to get their money back by smothering a young boy to death, and were apprehended doing so.

SUNDAY 18th MARCH 2007

John Collins' Hibs side thrashed Kilmarnock 5-1 in a breathtaking display in front of a full-house at Hampden Park to win the League Cup, the Easter Road side's first major trophy since 1991. Hibs' goals came from Steven Fletcher (2), Benji (2) and skipper Rob Jones. Gordon Greer got Kilmarnock's futile consolation. A moving spectacle after the match saw over 30,000 jubilant Hibs fans sing along to 'Sunshine On Leith' beneath the grey Hampden sky.

FRIDAY 19th MARCH 1948

Experimental summer running of Edinburgh's all-night bus service was sanctioned by the Public Utilities Committee to ascertain the need for them after the normal running period expired that month. The transport manager was asked to prepare a report on the possibility of including the night of Sunday/Monday in the schedule.

WEDNESDAY 20th MARCH 1935

Considerable damage to valuable stocks of wood was caused by a fire in the timber yard of Scott Morton and Tynecastle Company, adjoining the Albert Works of the firm in Murieston Road. Fortunately, the outbreak was confined to a section of the woodyard. The main building, in addition to several big sheds of wood, was entirely unaffected by the fire. The loss to the firm, which specialised in structural woodwork and carving in rare timbers, was estimated at several thousands of pounds. Although the firemen had the outbreak under their control within a short time, bringing half a dozen hoses from two engines to fight the flames, they were engaged for several hours in pulling down the planks of charred wood, which had to be watched very carefully. Hundreds of people, some of them half naked, hurried to the scene, and watched the flames shooting high into the air.

MONDAY 21st MARCH 1639

Amid the gathering clouds of civil war, Edinburgh Castle fell to a government force under General Alexander Leslie. The outer gate was demolished with a gunpowder charge and two inner gates broken down by the attackers, at which point the garrison promptly surrendered.

MONDAY 21st MARCH 2005

A teenager connected to a UVF loyalist drug gang appeared in court. It was alleged he had repeatedly stabbed a grandmother, and beat a pensioner senseless, in a day of terror in the capital in 2004. The 15-year-old, who had a history of drug addiction, attacked the 59-year-old grandmother in her home before, hours later, viciously attacking a 68-year-old man with his own walking stick. Both victims suffered potentially life-threatening injuries in the attacks and were left scarred. The 15-year-old could not be named for legal reasons, but had close connections to a drugs gang which tried to impose a rule of terror on a city estate. The gang, which boasted of its links to UVF terrorists, tried to set up a drugs empire based in tower blocks in Wester Hailes. Several gang members were jailed in 2004 for drugs and firearm offences. Lord Kinclaven deferred sentence on the teenager until the next month for the preparation of reports. The boy would meanwhile be detained in a secure unit.

THURSDAY 22nd MARCH 1917

Francis Love, a fortune-teller based in Greenside Place, appeared at the City Police Court charged with 'pretending to tell fortunes by palmistry and cards with the intent to impose upon his majesty's subjects'. Police had earlier encouraged two of Love's customers to return for a second reading, which subsequently proved different from the first, though two of Mr Love's other customers said in court they always found her to be 'genuine and most trustworthy'.

WEDNESDAY 23rd MARCH 1927

A scathing letter was read at a meeting of a sub-committee of the Lord Provost's Committee of Edinburgh Town Council from the Secretary of the Scottish Protestant League calling upon the council to take steps to prevent the procession of 'the host' taking place in the public thoroughfares of the capital. The sub-committee decided to take no action and allowed the Catholic Men's Rally to go ahead.

SUNDAY 24th MARCH 1799

A Presbyterian clergyman, William Fitzsimmons helped four sick and emaciated French prisoners escape from Edinburgh Castle. The fugitives spent one night at Fitzsimmons' house before travelling to Leith in disguise, aided by Fitzsimmons and by locals who were sympathetic to the French Republican cause, and even more sympathetic to the plight of the four weak, starved men who were miles away from home. From Leith, the Frenchmen were ferried to Inchkeith Island before managing to take a ship to the Netherlands and ultimately to freedom.

THURSDAY 24th MARCH 1859

The Scottish National Gallery opened after a gala reception and opening ceremony. It shared a building with the Royal Scottish Academy.

FRIDAY 25th MARCH 1708

A combined Franco-Jacobite fleet of 40 ships carrying James Stuart 'The Old Pretender' and 6,000 French, Scottish and Irish troops, unsuccessfully tried to stage a daring landing near Edinburgh. They were prevented from doing so by Admiral Byng and The Royal Navy Squadron patrolling the mouth of the Firth of Forth, with King James being refused permission to land alone by his French allies.

SUNDAY 25th MARCH 1810

The Commercial Bank of Scotland was founded in Edinburgh by John Pitcairn, Lord Cockburn and several others. The bank would become one of Scotland's greatest institutions until it eventually merged with RBS in the late 1960s.

WEDNESDAY 26th MARCH 1603

King James and Queen Anne were awoken from their sleep at Holyrood by a loud banging at the gates. A rider named Sir Robert Carey demanded to be taken straight to the king, whereupon he kneeled before James and gave him a ring, informing him that "Queen Elizabeth is dead and Your Majesty is now King of England." King James initially didn't believe the messenger, grumbling that "she has been dying for years anyway".

THURSDAY 26th MARCH 1936

The body of a woman, Isabel Ayer or Baker aged 49 from 31 Canongate, Edinburgh, was found in Duddingston Loch shortly before midday. The woman's body was seen in the water of the loch at a point opposite the boat-house by George Laidlaw, the park ranger. He drew her from the water and started artificial respiration, but without success. The body was taken in a police ambulance to the Royal Infirmary, where Isabel was pronounced dead upon arrival. Police were said to be 'making enquiries'.

MONDAY 27th MARCH 1871

Scotland played England at rugby for the first time. The match was played at Raeburn Place, and Scotland ran out winners by one goal and one try in front of 4,000 fans. There were 20 players on each team.

MONDAY 27th MARCH 1950

A worker at the SCWS at Chancelot Mills, Gosford Place, Leith, lost his left hand in an accident. Alex Elder, aged 40, of 13 Graham Street in Leith, was a machinist. While adjusting a belt in an elevator shaft his hand was caught in a loop of the belt. He was taken by ambulance, screaming in agony, to Leith Hospital where he was detained pending further examination.

MONDAY 28th MARCH 1927

With the beginning of a new roadway, an important stage was reached in the development of the project undertaken by the Edinburgh District Board of Control for the treatment of 'mental defectives' at Gogarburn. The new institution to be erected on the estate was to accommodate about a thousand patients, and while the Edinburgh District Board of Control oversaw the institution, it would be available for patients from the whole south-east of Scotland area. A beginning was to be made next month with the first part of the scheme, the completion of which, it was expected, would take about three years.

SATURDAY 29th MARCH 1783

The Royal Society of Edinburgh was formed by Royal Charter for 'the advancement of learning and useful knowledge and to seek to provide public benefit in today's Scotland'.

MONDAY 29th MARCH 1926

The Housing Committee of Edinburgh Town Council agreed to recommend that Saughtonhall Farm be purchased by the Corporation at a price of £175 per acre. The farm, which extended to about 214 acres, would be used for housing development, and it was also understood that the exclusion of Saughton golf course may also have been considered.

WEDNESDAY 29th MARCH 1950

Edinburgh University golfers, who had not won the title since 1939, opened with a strong bid in the first day's play of the Scottish Universities' Team Championship at Carnoustie. They defeated St Andrews, last year's winners, by five games to two, with three halved. The Edinburgh team's W Wood played a far from ignoble part by securing a square match after being three down with five to play.

THURSDAY 30th MARCH 1944

The Lord Provost's Committee of Edinburgh Town Council agreed to the construction of an industrial zone at Sighthill. This meant the council were definitely reserving over 130 acres of land for industry. City officials were to plan details of what would be an industrial estate and to submit their proposals at an early date. A large part of the area had also been reserved for housing development with suitable open spaces for recreation.

THURSDAY 30th MARCH 1989

The Scottish Constitutional Convention was held for the first time, in the Church of Scotland General Assembly Hall. Representatives from Labour, the Lib Dems, Green Party, trade unions, churches and even some businesses, met to sign the Claim of Right, asserting Scotland's right to self-determination and forming a basic blueprint for future devolution. The convention was boycotted by the SNP, and by the Tory party for ideological reasons.

SUNDAY 31st MARCH 1689

Furious at losing a court case that saw him forced to cough up for his ten children by his estranged wife, John Chiesley of Edinburgh took matters into his own hands and shot dead the presiding judge Sir John Lockhart with a duelling pistol, in front of hundreds of witnesses.

MONDAY 31st MARCH 1941

Trespassing on allotments resulted in three men appearing at Edinburgh Sheriff Court. It was stated that they were the first prosecutions of the kind heard in the city, and the men were admonished. In each case it was pointed out by the Depute-Fiscal that the men had not walked over tilled ground, but round the verges. Sheriff Robertson pointed out the accused were each liable to a fine of £50 under the defence regulations.

APRIL

TUESDAY 1st APRIL 1890

It was stated to a deputation from Edinburgh, which waited on the Caledonian Railway directors, that it had been resolved to construct a much needed, brand new railway station on the existing westward line to accommodate the people living in the Dalry suburb of the city.

SATURDAY 1st APRIL 1989

Nearly 20,000 angry city marchers from every political viewpoint took to the streets in unison to protest against the unfair Poll Tax on the day it was first introduced. One of the main gripes was that as well as the tax itself being unfair and expensive, the Conservative government were using Scotland as a 'guinea pig' to test the tax's impact before introducing it in the rest of the UK.

SUNDAY 2nd APRIL 1916

A German L-14 Zeppelin airship wrought havoc on Leith and Edinburgh by dropping high explosive and incendiary bombs at various locations, killing ten civilians and injuring many more. The airship's captain was a former sailor, who knew Edinburgh and Leith well.

SUNDAY 2nd APRIL 2006

With neither side able to sell their full ticket allocation because of the Sky TV-imposed Sunday lunch-time kick-off, 43,000 Hibs and Hearts fans were at Hampden to watch the Scottish Cup semi-final. Hearts led 1-0 at half-time thanks to a goal from Paul Hartley. Hibs had Ivan Sproule and Gary Smith red-carded in the second half, and two more goals from Hartley, and a strike by Edgar Jankauskas, crushed nine-man Hibs, who had been forced to field a weakened team because of injuries, suspensions and the departure of Garry O'Connor. It finished Hearts four, Hibs nil. Unstoppable Hearts would face second division Gretna in the final.

FRIDAY 3rd APRIL 1931

An item in *SPEED*, a monthly travel journal issued by the Corporation Transport Department, recommended using the tramcar network to go sightseeing in the capital. Suggested places of interest included Colinton Dell and Spylaw Park, which the journal claimed were 'away from the beaten track and of great charm'.

MONDAY 3rd APRIL 1950

The Forth ferry boat *Robert the Bruce* ran aground on a mudbank under the Forth Bridge at the South Queensferry side and the service was held up for two hours. On reaching Hawes Pier after the first trip of the day, a rope thrown ashore dropped short, and before the engines could be restarted a strong wind blew the boat on to the shore. After the nearby Queen Margaret had unloaded her passengers an attempt was made to tow the stranded vessel clear, but the rope broke. The turn of the tide was awaited before a second, successful, attempt.

MONDAY 4th APRIL 1689

The Scottish Parliament met in Edinburgh and ratified their earlier decision that James VII had forfeited the Scottish throne, following his flight to France after the Dutch invasion of England the previous November.

SATURDAY 5th APRIL 1603

King James VI left Edinburgh for London to take up his new role as king of 'Magna Britannia' following the death of England's Queen Elizabeth, unifying the crowns of Scotland and England.

MONDAY 6th APRIL 1931

Chief Traffic Officer Roy reported to the Edinburgh Safety First Council that there had been a small decrease in accidents compared to the same time last year. In total, five people were killed and 177 people injured in the preceding 12 months. Baillie Couston complimented the police on their work in reducing fatalities and also recommended the public should be advised not to step off the pavement with their backs to traffic.

TUESDAY 7th APRIL 1896

The new Royal Observatory on Blackford Hill was opened by Lord Balfour, Secretary of State. It was designed and equipped under the supervision of the new Astronomer Royal for Scotland, Ralph Copeland. The site included the new residence of the Astronomer Royal. Site, materials, buildings and embellishments were all carefully selected to provide a public monument to astronomy, as well as a state-of-the-art research centre.

MONDAY 7th APRIL 1941

Edinburgh suffered one of its most devastating air raids of the war when two giant mines were dropped on Leith by the Luftwaffe. Leith Town Hall's roof was destroyed, a church hall was badly damaged and the infant annexe of David Kilpatrick School was destroyed. Tenements in Largo Place were also hit, with several residents being killed. In total, 200 shops and 270 houses were damaged, along with three churches.

WEDNESDAY 8th APRIL 1936

"Edinburgh is the dirtiest city I have seen, with one exception," said author Eric Linklater, when he opened the cake, candy, and work sale in aid of the funds of the Edinburgh Nationalist Club and the Edinburgh Branch of the Scottish National party at 44a Hanover Street, Edinburgh. It was the dirtiest city he had seen, with the exception of the ancient Chinese city of Soochow. The author also produced research that showed Edinburgh had the largest canine population in the UK.

SATURDAY 8th APRIL 1995

Hopes for an all-Edinburgh Scottish Cup Final were dashed when Hearts lost their semi-final to Airdrieonians 1-0, Steve Cooper scoring for the Diamonds in front of a crowd of 22,000.

TUESDAY 9th APRIL 1940

A retired civil servant died in Edinburgh Royal Infirmary overnight as the result of an accident during the black-out. He was John Alexander, aged 68, of 16 Keir Street, Edinburgh. Walking in Lauriston Place on the night of March 27th, he collided with a woman pedestrian. He fell to the ground, and received a fracture of the right leg. Infection and other complications meant that he never recovered.

SATURDAY 9th APRIL 2005

Tony Mowbray's high flying Hibs side crashed out of the Scottish Cup, losing 2-1 to Dundee United at Hampden. Hibs took the lead with a Derek Riordan penalty early in the second half, but United hit back soon afterwards with two goals in three minutes from McIntyre and Scotland.

SATURDAY 10th APRIL 1999

Scotland beat France 36-22 in Paris to win the last ever Five Nations Championship after a heroic display in the Stade de France, England's defeat to Wales in London that weekend ensuring the Scots won the title. Scotland's management hailed the fans who had supported the side in the home fixtures at Murrayfield.

SUNDAY 10th APRIL 2005

Hearts faced a lunchtime kick-off in their Scottish Cup semi-final with Celtic at Hampden. The referee had to abandon a minute's silence for the deceased Pope John Paul II after a section of the Hearts support jeered and shouted sectarian abuse during the tribute. Celtic won the match 2-1, Cesnuaskis netting a late consolation for the Jambos.

SATURDAY 11th APRIL 1705

Captain Green, commander of an English ship named *The Worcester*, was executed in Edinburgh for piracy after his vessel was seized, and its cargo confiscated, in the Firth of Forth. Scotland's behaviour concerning this incident was agitated by England's series of threats to do similar things to Scottish vessels and trade under her own Parliament's 'Aliens Act'.

FRIDAY 11th APRIL 1947

Among the petitions granted by Edinburgh Dean of Guild Court was one by the superintendent of the Association for the Improvement of the Condition of the Poor in Leith, on behalf of the Leith Destitute Sick Society.

FRIDAY 12th APRIL 1935

At Edinburgh Burgh Court, fines of 5s each were imposed by Baillie Mrs Somerville on eight shopkeepers who admitted having illegally employed children between the ages of 12 and 14 for the delivery of milk after 8.30 on a Sunday morning, contrary to the local by-laws.

MONDAY 12th APRIL 1999

Edinburgh businessman and philanthropist Tom Farmer completed the sale of his successful Edinburgh-based nationwide Kwik-Fit automotive repairs business, selling it to US car giant Ford for a whopping £1 bn.

MONDAY 13th APRIL 1942

Edinburgh Accident Prevention Council met with the Police Chief Constable and decided blackout restrictions on Waverley Steps would not be relaxed, though smaller, shaded lights were being considered as replacements for the old ones due to a number of minor accidents.

TUESDAY 13th APRIL 1948

So far, Leith, which was an important coal-exporting centre before the war, had had a small part in the re-introduction of coal shipping to the Continent. It was reported that the steamer *Mania* would be loaded 'within the next week or so' with 1,000 tonnes of coal for Sweden. A notable arrival at Leith was also the steamer *Halifax County*, which brought 7,000 tons of oats from Australia. It was the second cargo of Australian oats received at the port within a fortnight.

SUNDAY 14th APRIL 1560

Twenty-seven English artillery pieces began bombarding the star-shaped artillery fort in Leith, in which were garrisoned some 2,000 French troops, sent to Scotland to back up Mary of Guise's regency. As part of the second Treaty of Berwick, the combined force of English soldiers, and the forces of the Scots' nobility, settled down for what was hoped would be a short, decisive siege.

SATURDAY 14th APRIL 1582

The University of Edinburgh was founded in the capital. The institution remains operational to this day, teaching home-grown and foreign students alike.

THURSDAY 15th APRIL 1954

John 'Uncle Paddy' Lynch became the third person to be hanged at Saughton Prison after he was convicted of the rape and murder of two children, four-year-old Lesley Nisbet and three-year-old Margaret Curran. Lynch had strangled the girls with a stocking in a public toilet and was caught when the woman he lived with noticed that one of her stockings was missing. It had earlier taken the jury at the High Court only 55 minutes to reach a unanimous 'guilty' verdict.

WEDNESDAY 16th APRIL 1746

At the Battle of Culloden, John Roy Stewart's Edinburgh regiment on the Jacobite side was wiped out, virtually to the last man. The 200 or so men of differing faiths had fought in the centre of Prince Charles' line.

SUNDAY 16th APRIL 1989

Alex Miller's Hibernian side was easily brushed aside by Celtic in the Scottish Cup semi-final at Hampden, losing three goals in the opening phase of the match. Steve Archibald netted Hibs' consolation effort in the second half.

TUESDAY 17th APRIL 1341

Scottish troops under Sir William Douglas managed to recapture Edinburgh Castle from the English using a cunning, but effective, ploy. Douglas himself pretended to be a merchant and approached the castle gates with a view of selling his wares to the garrison. When the English opened the gates, the Scots jammed them open then rushed in and reclaimed the castle with ruthless efficiency.

THURSDAY 17th APRIL 1766

James Craig's winning design entry for the radical development of Edinburgh New Town was finally approved.

SATURDAY 17th APRIL 2010

A schoolboy football match was abandoned after violent clashes broke out on the touchlines between gangs of youths armed with golf clubs and metal poles. Up to 40 rival gang members descended on the under-16 league match between Lochend Youth FC and Duddingston-based Cavalry Park at the pitches in Seafield. The match had to be abandoned at half-time after some of the youths produced weapons, many of which were salvaged from a nearby council dump, and staged a running battle.

MONDAY 18th APRIL 1921

The Scottish Motor Traction Company began, for the first time, a road and river tour from Edinburgh to Stirling. The business owned two motor yachts, and passengers made the journey by water, and then returned by road, or vice-versa if they so chose.

SATURDAY 18th APRIL 1992

The final performance at the Grassmarket, Edinburgh premises of the Traverse Theatre Company – 25 years after it was opened by Jenny Lee, Britain's first Minister of the Arts. The theatre re-opened at a custom-made building beside the Usher Hall.

WEDNESDAY 19th APRIL 1995

Hearts took a giant step towards avoiding relegation by beating Celtic 1-0 at Hampden Park, Celtic's temporary home, thanks to a late strike by ex-Rangers player David Hagen. Hearts' goalkeeper Craig Nelson was the hero, keeping the Hoops out time and time again with his heroics, much to the delight of the 200-odd Hearts fans who had made the trip along the M8. Hearts ended the season in sixth place, with Hibs finishing third.

TUESDAY 20th APRIL 1937

A middle-aged Edinburgh man, who assaulted his wife with a hatchet inflicting a fracture of the skull and other serious injuries 'to the danger of her life', was remitted for sentence to the High Court of Justiciary by Sheriff Jamieson at Edinburgh Sheriff Court. The accused was Michael Tansey, in custody, and the charge, which he admitted, bore that on March 5th, in the house at 27 Lochend Gardens occupied by Christina Tanseyhis, his wife, he did assault his wife and strike her a number of blows on the head and body with a hatchet, whereby she sustained a fracture of her skull and other serious injuries. Tansey also admitted that, by means of a poker or other instrument, he forced open the money container of a gas meter in the house and stole 4s 11d. Two previous convictions for offences inferring personal violence, both for breach of the peace and assault, and a conviction for breach of the peace, were also admitted by Tansey. No statements were made by the Fiscal or the agent who appeared for Tansey.

THURSDAY 20th APRIL 1972

City magistrates today granted a special licence for an all-night programme of horror films to be shown at the Odeon Cinema on May 20th, the first event of its kind in Scotland. Admission would be £1.

SATURDAY 21st APRIL 1703

After much planning, Edinburgh Fire Brigade was officially formed, one of the first forces of its kind in Scotland.

SUNDAY 22nd APRIL 1838

The 703-ton *Sirius*, built in Leith and carrying 90 passengers, reached New York, the first ship to cross the Atlantic entirely under steam. Shortage of fuel resulted in spars and furniture being burned towards the end of the 18-day voyage from Leith, which had stopped off in Liverpool.

FRIDAY 22nd APRIL 1910

Twenty men were charged at Edinburgh Burgh Court with spitting from cable-cars in the city. Each man was fined five shillings, which one of the accused described as 'pretty stiff' as he had merely been clearing his throat.

TUESDAY 23rd APRIL 1889

An angry meeting took place in George Street as the Lord Provost, and the few who supported him, discussed ways of protesting the day's announcement that the Irish civil rights activist and home-rule advocate Charles Stewart Parnell had been given the freedom of the city.

MONDAY 23rd APRIL 1956

Jubilant Hearts fans lined the streets of Edinburgh for a victory parade following the weekend's 3-1 win over Celtic in the cup final at Hampden. The Jambos dispatched Raith Rovers in a semi-final replay in front of over 54,000 fans at the city's other football stadium, Easter Road. A single mounted policeman rode in front of the open topped bus to prevent the vehicle from being swamped.

WEDNESDAY 23rd APRIL 1986

A 43-year-old blind woman from Granton was subjected to a horrific ordeal by a callous robber. The man broke in to her house and stole a cassette player, some cash and two rings, one of which was on his victim's finger. The robber threatened to tie the woman up if she did not keep quiet. Detectives on the trail of the robber labelled the incident 'hideous and cowardly'.

SUNDAY 24th APRIL 1558

The great cannon, Mons Meg, belched fire and spewed stone for the last time when it was fired in celebration of the marriage of a very young Mary, Queen of Scots, to the heir to the French throne, the Dauphin Francois.

TUESDAY 24th APRIL 2007

Hibs blew their chances of winning both of Scotland's major cup competitions in the same season when they lost their Scottish Cup semi-final replay to Dunfermline Athletic at Hampden Park in front of barely 7,000 fans. Jim McIntyre scored the only goal of the game with a coolly taken late penalty in the match's closing minutes, meaning that the Easter Road men would have to be happy with winning only one trophy.

WEDNESDAY 25th APRIL 1934

For several years, proposals to establish an airport in Edinburgh had been brought forward from time to time, but so far nothing had been accomplished. Edinburgh still remained without a civic landing ground for aircraft and from all the signs the day may not be far away when Edinburgh would be left rather lacking in the aerial running if she ignored the importance of the provision of a municipal aerodrome. As the leader of a deputation of businessmen to the Lord Provost's Committee of Edinburgh Town Council remarked, in effect, today, the capital may shortly find itself 'like a town or village which is left untouched by traffic after a by-pass road is constructed.'

SATURDAY 26th APRIL 1902

Hibernian defeated Celtic 1-0 to win the Scottish Cup in front of just over 16,000 fans in Glasgow, thanks to a goal by Andrew McGeachan.

FRIDAY 27th APRIL 1296

King John Balliol's Royal Scottish Army was routed by Edward I's superior English force at Spottsmuir, near Dunbar. Only one Scottish knight was killed, though many of the ordinary Scots foot-soldiers were not so lucky. The only thing left standing between the English and Stirling was now the undermanned, terrified garrison of Edinburgh Castle.

HEARTS PLAYERS CELEBRATE BEATING GRETNA IN THE 2006 CUP FINAL

SATURDAY 27th APRIL 1935

A huge demonstration by the Protestant Action Society over the council's decision to give a civic reception to the Catholic Young Men's Society of Britain passed without major incident in the High Street, though some bottles and fireworks were thrown by a 'minority of troublemakers'. Men wearing orange or red, white and blue rosettes filled the thoroughfare, and there were a few arrests.

SUNDAY 28th APRIL 1717

Robert Irvine, a home tutor who tried to sexually assault the maid at the home of two young boys that he taught in Broughton, decided to take his revenge on the two youngsters as they had informed others about his attack. When their parents were out, he took the two boys up Multrie's Hill and slit their throats. He was seen doing so, and was overpowered just after he had tried to compound his sin by adding suicide to murder by cutting his own throat. He was thrown into the tollbooth with his gaping throat wound left untended until he could be executed.

MONDAY 28th APRIL 1998

A deal was announced today to secure the go-ahead for the £62 million North Edinburgh Waterfront development, creating 4,000 jobs in Scotland's largest urban regeneration project. The old gasworks, which covered 70 acres at Granton, had been sold to the City of Edinburgh Council for £3 million. Owner BG Property Division (formerly British Gas) was to share the cost of cleaning up the site with Lothian and Edinburgh Enterprise (LEEL). The deal fulfilled a long-standing plan by the local authority to develop Granton which began nearly ten years previously with the compulsory purchase of derelict land. The site, which was the size of the New Town, had been the subject of considerable degradation through industrial development over the last century. The sale did not affect the Scottish Gas offices which would continue to be based at Granton.

SUNDAY 29th APRIL 1990

South Queensferry's Stephen Hendry, aged 21, became the youngest ever world snooker champion by beating Jimmy White 18-12 in a thrilling final.

MONDAY 30th APRIL 1928

The Anchor liner *Transylvania*, which had arrived at Princes Dock, Glasgow, from New York, had on board a cargo of snakes for the Scottish Zoo at Edinburgh. Included among the reptiles were two fine specimens of Gila monsters, one of them being 14 feet in length. The creatures were delivered to the zoo at lunchtime.

FRIDAY 30th APRIL 1999

Russian tall ship the *Sedov* made a welcome return to Leith to help celebrate the first anniversary of the Royal Yacht *Britannia's* arrival in the port. The *Sedov* was the world's biggest sailing ship and had last visited Leith in 1995 for the Tall Ships Race. The mighty vessel was built from trees felled in the Siberian wilderness.

MAY

SUNDAY 1st MAY 1927

Only a few citizens of Edinburgh honoured the old custom of going 'A-Maying' on this morning. This was not due to any unwillingness on the part of those who wanted to wash their faces in May dew and thus secure beauty, but to the fact that instead of the traditional dew of May morning there was actually a considerable coating of snow on the ground. Arthur's Seat, which was the favourite destination of the May morning parties, was almost deserted, only a few enthusiasts climbing to the top.

THURSDAY 1st MAY 1997

Scotland spoke in the General Election, ejecting every single Conservative MP including Foreign Secretary Malcolm Rifkind, who lost his Edinburgh Pentlands seat amid the Labour landslide. Edinburgh-born Tony Blair became the UK's new Prime Minister.

SATURDAY 2nd MAY 1998

Hibs lost 2-1 at home to Dundee United and were relegated from the Scottish Premier League, despite a revival in fortunes since the appointment of Alex McLeish as manager that had almost saved them from the drop. Two second-half goals from Kjell Olofsson were enough to sink Hibs, despite Grant Brebner's deflected opener in the first half.

MONDAY 3rd MAY 1926

Under the slogan of 'Not a penny off the pay – not a minute on the day', and amid widespread public sympathy, workers in Edinburgh joined their comrades and workers across the country in Britain's General Strike. Local co-operatives had lowered the price of bread, and all of the city's pubs were closed.

SATURDAY 3rd MAY 1986

Hearts threw away the league title on the last day of the season, losing 2-0 to Dundee at Dens Park when a mere draw would have been enough to clinch the title for the Jambos. Celtic won the title after thrashing St Mirren 5-0 at Love Street to win the league on goal difference. Dundee's goals were scored by substitute Albert Kidd.

MONDAY 4th MAY 1936

Two men, who were arrested at the Mound on Sunday night, where there was a considerable violent disturbance during a fascist meeting, were brought before Baillie Coltart at Edinburgh Burgh Court, and remitted to the Sheriff Court. The men were James Sutherland of 12 Queen's Place, Edinburgh, and Robert Robertson of 27 South Street in Musselburgh. Sutherland was charged that on Sunday, at the Mound, he formed part of a disorderly crowd, conducted himself in a disorderly manner, threw stones to the danger of the lieges, and committed a breach of the peace. The charge against Robertson was that at the Mound, also on Sunday, he formed part of a disorderly crowd, conducted himself in a disorderly manner and committed a breach of the peace. He also assaulted a police constable while in the execution of his duty, and struck him on the chest. No plea was taken in either case.

TUESDAY 5th MAY 1942

The Boy Scouts Association announced the chief scout had awarded the Silver Cross to Gordon Stewart, a patrol leader of the 1st Craiglockhart Scout Troop, who, at grave risk to his life, saved Joyce Mackintosh, a 15-year-old girl, from drowning when the ice on which she was skating gave way and she and a friend fell into the icy water.

FRIDAY 5th MAY 1995

Meadowbank Thistle played their last-ever game at Meadowbank Stadium before their imminent move to Livingston where they were to be 'refranchised' as Livingston FC. Already relegated to Division Three, they won their final home game, beating Stenhousemuir 1-0.

TUESDAY 6th MAY 1930

A remarkable tragedy occurred in Leith, the victim being a 17-year-old butcher's apprentice, James Campbell of 2 Portland Terrace. In a report on the circumstances of the tragedy, the police stated that the deceased quarrelled with his brother, and in a fit of passion ran out of the house. On arriving at Bernard Street Bridge he climbed on to the parapet and threw himself into the harbour. The dead body was recovered after spending about an hour in the water.

WEDNESDAY 6th MAY 1953

A baby was born at the city's Queen Mary Maternity Home, his full name being Anthony Charles Lynton Blair.

WEDNESDAY 7th MAY 1924

The Rev. William Main, Clerk to the Presbytery of Edinburgh, and the Rev. Dr Burns, representing the Presbytery of Edinburgh, had a meeting with Lord Provost Sleigh with regard to the question of the increase in the number of irregular marriages in the town. In the course of this meeting they explained the churches had come to an arrangement, in virtue of which they hoped that greater facilities for the celebration of regular marriages would be given. They trusted the result of this would be a decrease in the number of irregular marriages in the future.

MONDAY 7th MAY 1945

Some of Edinburgh's citizens 'jumped the gun' by starting their VE celebrations a day early, with huge bonfires made of stored-up rubbish springing up around the capital. Several men were arrested for being drunk and incapable, while another man was arrested for discharging a pistol into the air.

THURSDAY 8th MAY 1924

Mr J Inglis Kerr, the well-known authority on Scottish roads, made a radio broadcast regarding the proposed road bridge across the Forth at Queensferry. He reminded listeners that such plans were nothing new, and had actually been in existence since 1918. Inglis noted that a steamboat service could never be a long-term solution, and claimed a new bridge would never be used by more than 2,000 vehicles in one day, and would be free from tolls.

TUESDAY 8th MAY 1945

The Royal Mile was decked out with bunting and every Allied flag as the city celebrated VE day, with street parties springing up everywhere across the city, including one in Stockbridge specifically for children. The capital's celebrations were emulated nationwide, with similarly joyous celebrations in all of Scotland's major cities.

TUESDAY 9th MAY 1911

The world renowned illusionist Lafayette, and nine others, were killed backstage in a blaze at the Empire Palace Theatre in Nicholson Street, after a lantern fell onto the stage and set fire to the scenery. The 3,000 attendees were lucky, being safely evacuated within three minutes. A number of wild beasts also perished in the inferno.

THURSDAY 9th MAY 1918

John MacLean, the socialist revolutionary and first Soviet Consul in Britain in 1917, and also the honorary president of the first Congress of Soviets, was tried in the High Court in Edinburgh for sedition. He was sentenced to five years in Peterhead Prison.

FRIDAY 10th MAY 1935

George Davidson (40), of 40 Jewel Cottages, Portobello, was injured by a fall of coal while he was busy working in the Woolmit Pit this morning. He was conveyed to the Edinburgh Royal Infirmary, suffering from an abdominal injury and concussion, where it was hoped he would make a full recovery. The cause of the fall was yet to be established.

SATURDAY 10th MAY 1986

Having thrown away the league title by failing to beat Dundee in the last league game of the season a week previously, Hearts faced Aberdeen in the Scottish Cup Final at Hampden, looking to win some silverware to reward their otherwise impressive season. Aberdeen won the match 3-0 with two goals from John Hewitt and a strike from Billy Stark. Many would-be entrepreneurs were left with vast hoards of 'Hearts Double Winners 1986' T-shirts.

FRIDAY 11th MAY 1928

Edinburgh Fire Brigade were called out to two outbreaks of fire. One occurred in a gravel yard at Pilrig Street, belonging to William Swan. A small wooden building used as a tool shed, and its contents, were destroyed. Two engines were out, and the outbreak was extinguished in about an hour. The brigade was also later called to West House, the Royal Edinburgh Insane Asylum, where a wooden erection 50 feet by 20 feet, used as a storeroom for fodder and for incubators, caught fire. Eleven incubators and 20 tons of fodder were destroyed.

FRIDAY 12th MAY 1916

Edinburgh-born trade unionist, civil rights activist and Hibernian fan James Connolly was executed in Dublin for his part in commanding Dublin's GPO during the failed Easter Rising. Connolly had been so badly wounded in the battle that British soldiers had to tie him to a chair so he could face his firing squad.

WEDNESDAY 12th MAY 1926

The General Strike officially ended and most of Edinburgh went back to work, though not without incident. Shop windows in the High Street and on North Bridge were smashed amid riotous looting and police were forced to resort to baton charges to restore order.

THURSDAY 13th MAY 1999

Labour MP Donald Dewar was duly elected as First Minister for the newly devolved Scottish Parliament in Edinburgh, the first man to hold such a position in any way, shape or form since the early 18th century.

SATURDAY 13th MAY 2006

A huge Hearts support dwarfed the opposing support at Hampden as Heart of Midlothian won the Scottish Cup by beating second division Gretna 4-2 on penalties after the sides had been evenly matched at 1-1 after extra-time. Hearts' semi-final hero Paul Hartley was sent off in the dying minutes of the match. Gavin Skelton missed the decisive penalty for Gretna.

SUNDAY 14th MAY 1933

The destroyers of the 2nd, 4th, and 6th Flotillas lying in the Forth provided entertainment for hundreds of visitors from Edinburgh, Glasgow, and other parts of Scotland. It was the Navy's show day, and the destroyers deserved all the admiration bestowed upon them. Early that morning the 2nd and 6th Flotillas slipped quietly out to sea to take part in gun-firing practice, torpedo attacks, and mine sweeping exercises. They would be joined on Wednesday by the 5th Flotilla, and all three flotillas would return at the end of the week. Despite the keenness of the crews, there would hardly be time for boat practice before the regatta, after which the destroyers would proceed to the Moray Firth for Fleet exercises.

SUNDAY 15th MAY 2005

The heart of Edinburgh was made car-free in one of the biggest changes to traffic management in the city for 40 years. All cars, apart from taxis, would be diverted from the westbound side of Princes Street between 7am and 8pm daily, a measure applied to the eastbound side in 1996. The scheme, which affected nearly 40 streets, gave pedestrians and cyclists priority on George Street. City leaders said about 30% of traffic was passing through and causing congestion, instead of contributing to the economy. A number of roads in the New Town were also blocked off, with traffic diverted on to routes such as Queen Street.

SATURDAY 16th MAY 1942

St Bernard's, one of five Edinburgh clubs in the Scottish Football League, played their last-ever match before being consigned to the history books. They lost 3-2 to East Fife at Eyre Place in Edinburgh.

SATURDAY 16th MAY 1998

Hearts ended their near 50-year trophyless run by beating Rangers 2-1 at Celtic Park to lift the Scottish Cup. An early penalty from Colin Cameron, and a second-half strike from Stephane Adam, were enough to bring the cup back to Gorgie, despite a late goal by Rangers' Ally McCoist.

SUNDAY 17th MAY 1998

Hearts fans packed the streets of Edinburgh for an open-top bus parade by their victorious Scottish Cup-winning side. One of the biggest crowds of spectators ever seen on the streets of the capital basked both in sunshine and glory.

MONDAY 18th MAY 1931

The usual Victoria Day bonfires caused a very busy evening for the Edinburgh Fire Brigade, which received 45 calls. All the machines in the city were out at different times, and in some stations all the available fire engines were unavailable. The damage in most cases consisted of window panes cracked by heat, woodwork scorched and in many cases a line of hose had to be used to extinguish the bonfires. In Leith a number of minor accidents occurred, and about a dozen people, adults and children, had to be attended to at Leith Hospital for burns, most of which were caused by the setting-off of fireworks.

SATURDAY 18th MAY 1996

Hearts were crushed 5-1 at Hampden in the Scottish Cup Final by champions Rangers. Ex-Hibs striker Gordon Durie bagged a hat-trick for the Govan side, whose other two goals were scored by Brian Laudrup. John Colquhoun netted Hearts' goal in the second half.

THURSDAY 19th MAY 1927

In the House of Commons, Mr Saklatvaw MP (Con, Battersea North) asked the Secretary of State for Scotland whether his attention had been called to the fact that certain restaurants in Edinburgh were refusing admission to Asiatic and African residents, not because of any complaints against their conduct, which was admitted to be unexceptionable, but purely on account of their racial origin, and whether he would take steps, by legislation or otherwise, to remove this form of discrimination against a section of His Majesty's subjects.

MONDAY 19th MAY 1947

The body of the woman found in the Pentland Hills near Balerno was identified as that of Dr Alice Margaret Ross, a graduate of Edinburgh University who was at one time in the Radiological Department of Edinburgh Royal Infirmary. Dr Ross was 35 years of age, and had been missing for more than a week from Mount Vernon Hospital, Northwood, Middlesex, where she was on the staff. She graduated in 1931 and became a Fellow of the Royal College of Surgeons, Edinburgh, in 1937.

SATURDAY 20th MAY 1649

James Graham, Marquis of Montrose and brilliant leader of Royal forces in Scotland during The War of the Three Kingdoms, arrived in Edinburgh at Leith as a prisoner, facing execution for treason – despite never having been given a trial for the crime. He had earlier led parliamentarian forces a merry dance with his mix-and-match force of Highlanders and Irishmen.

MONDAY 20th MAY 1991

Police in Edinburgh were treating a blaze that destroyed an infamous Stockbridge nightspot as 'suspicious'. Cinderellas Rockerfellas in St Stephen Street had to be demolished after being completely gutted by the fire.

THE PLAQUE IN THE COWGATE WHICH COMMEMORATES EDINBURGH'S WORKING-CLASS HERO AND REVOLUTIONARY, JAMES CONNOLLY

TO THE MEMORY OF JAMES CONNOLLY

BORN 5TH JUNE 1868 AT 107 COWGATE

RENOWNED INTERNATIONAL TRADE UNION

AND WORKING CLASS LEADER

FOUNDER OF IRISH SOCIALIST REPUBLICAN PARTY

MEMBER OF PROVISIONAL GOVERNMENT

OF IRISH REPUBLIC

EXECUTED 12TH MAY 1916 AT KILMAINHAM JAIL DUBLIN

FRIDAY 20th MAY 1994

Labour leader John Smith's funeral was held in Cluny Church, Morningside, following the untimely death of the man whom many saw as the Prime Minister in waiting. He had represented Monklands East in Lanarkshire prior to dying of a heart attack.

THURSDAY 21st MAY 1936

A peculiar case was heard in Edinburgh Burgh Court in which a young man, resident in the Granton district, was charged with having a loft in his garden, and with having kept a number of pigeons so as to be a nuisance and an annoyance to the residents next door 'by reason of the pigeons' persistent cooing and their dropping of excrement on the roof of the neighbour's house.' The prosecution was brought under a section of the Edinburgh Corporation Order, 1933. Giving judgment, the judge said he was not satisfied that the complaint levelled against the accused that the pigeons' behaviour constituted a nuisance had been proved, and he accordingly found the accused not guilty. The case was followed with interest by a number of societies interested in the breeding and racing of pigeons.

MONDAY 22nd MAY 1649

The Marquis of Montrose was executed by hanging at the city's Canongate. A huge crowd maintained a dignified silence throughout the proceedings, and the Marquis was said to have appeared 'more like a bridegroom than a condemned man'. Covenanter guards watched closely for any sign of a rescue attempt.

SATURDAY 22nd MAY 1915

Edinburgh's single biggest loss of life in the war occurred on home soil when 215 members of the 7th Leith Battalion of The Royal Scots were killed in a frightful rail crash at Gretna Junction. Twelve civilians were also killed in the tragic incident, as was Lieutenant Christian Salvesen, son of the globally renowned shipping magnate. The soldiers, many of whom were Irishmen, or Leith men of Irish descent, had been on their way to Liverpool where they were to set sail for the Dardanelles in Turkey. Three locomotives were involved in the crash, and only 89 of those killed were recognisable, the rest being badly burned or completely vaporised due to the inferno that engulfed the carriages.

MONDAY 23rd MAY 1927

At Edinburgh Sheriff Court, Sheriff Orr imposed a sentence of six weeks' imprisonment upon David Gray, a widower of 63 Broughton Road, Edinburgh, for neglecting his three children by failing to provide them with sufficient food, clothing, and bedding, and keeping them in dirty conditions. The case was the latest in a long line of actions against absentee fathers who refused to pay towards their children's upkeep.

THURSDAY 23rd MAY 1946

A three-year-old Edinburgh child, Maria Feeney, was electrocuted outside her home at 68 Grassmarket. She was found lying alongside an ARP shelter at the rear of her home clutching in her hand the flex of an electric cable which apparently was live. The cable led from an adjacent building to the ARP shelter, and had become loose.

THURSDAY 24th MAY 1945

An audience which included a number of American and Dominion servicemen, who were taking a special course at the University of Edinburgh, listened to a programme on 'The Forty-Five', relayed by means of loudspeaker to several rooms in the Scottish-American Centre in Regent Terrace, Edinburgh. The programme commemorated the bicentenary of the outbreak and was produced with the same technique as was the recent 'Defence of London'. Compiled by Mr H Harvey Wood and Mr Edwin Muir, it described the rising from the first landing, and concluded with the death of Prince Charles Edward in Rome. Use was made of incidental music, bagpipes and drums, and the text was based on contemporary documents. The sources included 'The Lyon in Mourning', broadsheets and proclamations, and the dramatic element was introduced by the use of authentic reported conversation of the period. The production was by Miss Lennox Milne and her assistants.

SATURDAY 25th MAY 1940

Following a national appeal by the Foreign Secretary Lord Halifax and a subsequent meeting in The Golfers Rest, Braid Hills, 'C' Company 3rd Edinburgh Home Guard was formed by volunteers from the Morningside and Blackford areas, with 50 men initially given responsibility for civilian defence in the Morningside District.

WEDNESDAY 25th MAY 1956

The General Assembly of the Church of Scotland was informed that random roadside breath tests on drivers could prevent many thousands of deaths and maimings on the roads every year. Rev John Peat, who presented the report to the Temperance and Moral Welfare Committee in Edinburgh, was delighted that a government White Paper had come along to address the issue.

FRIDAY 26th MAY 1424

The parliament convened by King James I in Edinburgh approved the arrest of a number of the Scottish nobility for treason, among other offences. They also banned the playing of football for fear it would lead to men spending less time becoming competent in the bearing of arms for national defence.

TUESDAY 26th MAY 1925

The Italian destroyers *Leone*, *Pantera*, and *Gigio* entered Edinburgh Dock and saluted the British Flag with 21 guns. During the afternoon a reply was fired from Edinburgh Castle's half-moon battery.

SATURDAY 26th MAY 2001

Hibs travelled to Hampden where they faced treble-chasing Celtic in the Scottish Cup Final. A woeful display by the Easter Road men saw them lose 3-0 to Martin O'Neil's team, whose scorers were Jackie McNamara and Henrik Larsson (2).

TUESDAY 27th MAY 1947

A newborn male infant was found by a gardener lying in a corner of Belgrave Crescent Gardens, Edinburgh, covered with two purple chiffon squares and a piece of purple serge cloth. He was taken to the Simpson Memorial Maternity Pavilion. The police believed the baby was between six and eight hours old when he was found.

SATURDAY 28th MAY 1329

Dying of leprosy in his bed at Cardross Castle, King Robert I managed to sign and seal a Royal Charter that granted his port at Leith to the burgesses of the Royal Burgh of Edinburgh. King Robert was not expected to live longer than a few more days.

THURSDAY 28th MAY 1573

Sir William Kirkcaldy of Grange's 18-month defence of Edinburgh Castle in the name of Queen Mary came to an end when The Earl of Mar, Regent, battered the castle into submission using an artillery train loaned to him by the English.

SUNDAY 28th MAY 1905

Construction of the new King's Theatre in Edinburgh commenced near the city's Tollcross area. The foundation stone was laid by an unknown local politician.

MONDAY 28th MAY 1979

After two goalless draws, Hibs took on Rangers in the Scottish Cup Final at Hampden, looking to win the second replay. Hibs lost the third and final game 3-2, Rangers' winning strike coming from an own-goal by Hibs' Arthur Duncan. 50,000 fans had watched the first match but barely 30,000 were there to see the tie finally decided.

WEDNESDAY 29th MAY 1992

An undercover investigation by the *Evening News* revealed a gang of professional beggars posing as homeless people were operating in the city centre. 'The blanket crew', as they were known, worked key spots at the east end of Princes Street, using a variety of scams to con the public. Earning £100 a day in some cases, the gang had been spotted changing into scruffy clothing before cowering under blankets. They even used a 'shift' system to maximise profits.

WEDNESDAY 30th MAY 1917

There came to light a distressing tragedy which had taken place in Edinburgh some time the previous Sunday. The dead bodies of a woman, Annie Grant or Wilmot, aged 32, and her children, William (aged four) and Charles (five months), were discovered in a top-flat house of a tenement at 120 Rose Street South Lane, a short distance from the west end of Princes Street, following the surrender to the police in Glasgow of the woman's husband, Joseph Wilmot, a fitter's labourer. During Monday and Tuesday the bodies had lain in the house unattended. The neighbours were not aware of what had occurred.

MONDAY 30th MAY 1949

Sentence of one year's imprisonment was imposed by Sheriff-Principal Sir John C Fenton KC at Edinburgh Sheriff Court today on Elizabeth Wilson Aitken or Lyall, aged 38, when she admitted two charges of having performed illegal operations on two women. It was stated by her counsel, Mr L Daiches, advocate, that the accused had committed the offences out of a mistaken sense of kindness. She had a hitherto impeccable character, and was a highly respected wife and mother.

MONDAY 31st MAY 1982

His Holiness Pope John Paul II touched down at Turnhouse Airport, kissing the tarmac as he disembarked on a visit to Edinburgh as part of his pastoral visit to the UK, amid tight security and even some controversy ahead of his meeting with Scotland's religious leaders, some of whom had actually written to Prime Minister Margaret Thatcher imploring her to block his visit in case it upset the Orange Order. It was the first-ever visit to the UK by a Pope.

FRIDAY 31st MAY 1991

Lothian Region Transport finally banned all smoking on buses to coincide with World No Smoking Day. Drivers would not be responsible for enforcing the ban but would radio for police assistance if they needed help after spotting offenders.

JUNE

MONDAY 1st JUNE 1936

An Edinburgh telegraph messenger was fatally injured as the result of an accident which occurred at Liberton shortly after one o'clock. The boy was 16-year-old James Hutchison of 51 Iona Street. He had been employed at the Edinburgh GPO for nearly two years. He was returning from delivering a telegram in Lasswade Road, when the cycle he was riding was involved in a collision with a motor car at the junction of Kirk Brae with Braefoot Terrace, at the bottom of Liberton Brae. Hutchison was badly injured about the head, and was treated in a chemist's shop within a few yards of the scene of the accident. He was then taken to the Royal Infirmary in an ambulance, but he died before arrival.

MONDAY 2nd JUNE 1924

A number of points which had caused delay in the progress of the Edinburgh-Glasgow road had now been settled, and the work was to proceed. The Special Committee of Edinburgh Town Council dealing with the scheme met on this day to consider the terms of the agreement between the Ministry of Transport and the Local Authorities. These were approved, and the Committee instructed the engineer to advertise for tenders for carrying out the work on the first section of the road at the Edinburgh end. Various points which were remitted to Mr A Grierson, Town Clerk of Edinburgh, had been adjusted satisfactorily, and the work, it was stated, would commence almost immediately.

MONDAY 3rd JUNE 1940

Edinburgh parents responded in a lesser degree than was expected to the appeal to register their children for eventual evacuation. Schools were opened on Saturday and again today for the purpose of registration, and as a result it has been computed that only from 20 to 25 per cent of the 47,000 Corporation schoolchildren still in the city were registered. There were already about 13,500 Edinburgh children in reception areas – 9,000 from Corporation schools, and 4,500 from Merchant Company and private schools. Between 25 and 30 per cent of Merchant Company scholars remaining in the city were registered by this weekend. Other children had been evacuated privately, and more were expected to be in due course. These figures indicate that of the 66,000 children attending school in Edinburgh, about half had been evacuated or registered for evacuation.

MONDAY 3rd JUNE 1946

A meeting attended by 2,500 people was held in the Usher Hall, Edinburgh, to protest against the proposed demobilisation in Scotland of the Polish forces. After hearing speeches by Councillor J Cormack of Edinburgh, and Councillor M S Sim, Inverkeithing, the meeting passed a resolution calling upon the Prime Minister to reconsider immediately his decision to send members of the Polish forces, with their wives and families, to settle in Scotland, as it was believed the majority of the people in Scotland did not want them here. They also urged that the Poles already in Scotland be given accommodation in ships to take them back to Poland as soon as could be arranged.

THURSDAY 4th JUNE 1818

Golfing history was made in the capital as the first recorded inter-club golf match between Edinburgh Burgess Golfing Society and Bruntsfield Links Golf Club was contested.

FRIDAY 4th JUNE 1999

Rolling Stones frontman Mick Jagger was disappointed when he tried to eat at an Italian restaurant in George Street. The head chef of Est. Est. Est sent Jagger and his companions to wait in a pub over the road as his restaurant was full, despite the rock star professing his desire to eat there because of its 'lively reputation'. Upon his return, Jagger, who was in town for his band's Murrayfield gig, decided not to eat at the restaurant as it lacked privacy.

MONDAY 5th JUNE 1093

Queen Margaret, the wife of King Malcolm Canmore King of Scots, and the woman whose 'Queen's Ferry' gave its name to two modern settlements on opposite banks of the River Forth, died in Edinburgh Castle.

FRIDAY 5th JUNE 1868

James Connolly was born to Irish immigrant parents in the city's Cowgate area, a district of extreme poverty and degradation that made a great impression on him and would eventually compel him to help lead an attempted Socialist revolution in Ireland. He was the son of a dung-carter and helped his father with his work.

WEDNESDAY 6th JUNE 1296

Flushed by their easy victory over the Scottish Royal army at Dunbar, the English army under King Edward I arrived in Edinburgh and began a five-day bombardment of the castle, using Greek fire and gigantic siege engines.

WEDNESDAY 6th JUNE 1934

A warning to Edinburgh butchers was given by Mrs Somerville at Edinburgh Burgh Court when Peter Braid, a butcher of 5 Seafield Road, Portobello, admitted a charge of having sold a pound of mince which contained a quantity of added preservative contrary to the Food and Drugs Adulteration Act of 1928. It was Braid's first offence and in view of his otherwise unblemished record he was fined £5.

THURSDAY 7th JUNE 1928

Injuries sustained in a fall from scaffolding in an Edinburgh church resulted in the death of John Dick, a joiner, residing at 2 Henderson Terrace. It appears that while Dick was engaged in taking measurements of the plasterwork of the ceiling of St Peter's Chapel in Falcon Avenue, the plank on which he was standing slipped, and he fell to the floor – a distance of 50 feet. He was conveyed to the Royal Infirmary by ambulance, but on arrival was found to be dead.

MONDAY 8th JUNE 1942

Before leaving Edinburgh in the morning, Her Majesty the Queen paid an informal visit to the Red Cross Shop in South Charlotte Street, accompanied by Lord and Lady Elphinstone, and took the greatest interest in all that she saw. That interest was no new thing. Prominently displayed were gifts sent by the Queen herself, by Queen Mary, and by Princess Elizabeth. The Queen remarked that her daughter's gift – a case for a needlewoman – "was the most utilitarian"!

FRIDAY 8th JUNE 1990

The capital had 451 redundancies in the first quarter of this year, its worst start to a year since 1986, according to today's edition of the city's economic and employment review, published by the district council.

SATURDAY 9th JUNE 1660

A 'Day of Public Thanksgiving' for the restoration of King Charles II to the throne was observed in Scotland, with Edinburgh's celebrations believed to have been the most boisterous. Several citizens died of 'over consumption'.

WEDNESDAY 9th JUNE 1926

A meeting of the Edinburgh Coal Emergency Committee was held in the City Chambers, when the situation was again reviewed. It was reported there was sufficient coal in hand for the needs of domestic consumers, and that there was very little demand for household coal at the present time. In the circumstances, it was agreed to carry on the usual lines meantime, that is, one bag per fortnight, per household.

WEDNESDAY 10th JUNE 1903

The famous floral clock in Princes Street Gardens, Edinburgh, began operating – driven by clockwork and with only an hour hand.

FRIDAY 10th JUNE 1955

Three young men were quizzed by Edinburgh cops after a woman had reported finding shattered pieces of the Greyfriars Bobby memorial fountain on the road. It had only recently been put back in place after it was damaged by a car collision. The men were released pending further investigation of what the *Edinburgh Evening News* described as 'malicious mischief'.

TUESDAY 11th JUNE 1560

Mary of Guise, the fearsome woman who became Queen-Consort of Scotland after becoming James V's second wife, and the mother of Mary Queen of Scots, died of 'dropsy' in Edinburgh Castle.

FRIDAY 11th JUNE 1915

Baillie Rose and Councillor Stewart, at a sitting of Edinburgh Burgh Court, granted licences to 32 women to act as conductors in the employment of Edinburgh Tramway Company. There were another six young women present, but they were married women whose husbands were at the front, or who were earning good wages at home, and it was decided to postpone consideration of their applications.

WEDNESDAY 12th JUNE 1974

Tons of scaffolding collapsed in Rose Street, right in front of hundreds of onlookers, trapping one man for 15 minutes before he was rescued by firemen and scaffolders. The structure and huge chunks of masonry fell some 85 feet to the ground, smashing shop windows and forcing emergency crews to conduct a thorough search of the rubble to ensure no-one else was trapped.

WEDNESDAY 12th JUNE 1990

Millionaire Tom Farmer came to the rescue of beleaguered Hibs by buying a 'substantial number' of Hibs shares in a bid to block Hearts chairman Wallace Mercer's unpopular takeover bid. Mr Farmer was keen to stress this was a blocking move with the sole intent of saving Hibs, rather than an attempt to take over the club himself. Mercer's bid had been met with great hostility from fans of both Edinburgh clubs, who hated the idea of the takeover. Mercer was sent human excrement and bullets in the post.

SUNDAY 13th JUNE 1926

With 'No More War' as their slogan, a section of the Peacemakers' Pilgrimage left Edinburgh for London, where they would take part in a peace demonstration in Hyde Park the next Saturday. The Pilgrims assembled at Charlotte Square, in the presence of a large crowd and, after a short meeting, continued their journey, a number of supporters walking part of the way with them. Most of the 20 women who set out were from Edinburgh. From Newcastle southward they would travel by rail.

THURSDAY 13th JUNE 1940

The Scottish National Zoological Park, Edinburgh, had lost several of its older inhabitants during the past year, and another of them had just been added to the sick list, 'Wellington' an old black-footed penguin. He was one of a pair of black-footed penguins, purchased early in 1919. As 'Wellington' advanced in years, he developed a curious growth upon his beak which, when viewed in profile, gave rise to his name. Wellington was in adult life when he arrived at the Park, and must, therefore, have been more than 22 years old when he died.

WEDNESDAY 14th JUNE 1944

The passing of more than 20 truckloads of German prisoners of war through the streets caught the attention of Edinburgh pedestrians who were provided with a dramatic reminder of the turn in the war tide. Many people stopped to watch the convoy go by; the prisoners, who were under the charge of armed guards and who appeared to be in good spirits wore, in the majority of cases, the dark brown suit with the blue circle stamped on the back, but field grey, Luftwaffe blue and navy blue were also seen among them. Some of the prisoners sang as they passed, pausing often to give the Nazi salute. Some of the men carried small posies of flowers.

SUNDAY 15th JUNE 1567

Queen Mary spent her last-ever night in Edinburgh, at the house of Sir Simon Preston, the Lord Provost, on the Royal Mile, prior to her impending imprisonment at Loch Leven castle.

WEDNESDAY 15th JUNE 1927

Effie Young, a girl of 16 from 20 Cowan Road, Edinburgh, had been detained in the Edinburgh Royal Infirmary suffering from shock, concussion and a broken wrist, as the result of a fall from the rocks of Craiglockhart Hill. The girl was apparently playing when she lost her footing and fell several dozen feet. Doctors had described her survival as 'miraculous'.

TUESDAY 16th JUNE 1936

The trial was continued before the Lord Justice-Clerk, and a jury in the High Court at Edinburgh, of two young men, Roderick Maxwell and Robert Edwards Gilchrist, on a charge of being concerned in the bank hold-up at Slamannan in December. It was alleged by the prosecution that the accused acted together, and with another person or other persons unknown, on December 16th 1935, and stole a motor car from Belford Road in Edinburgh. Then, at the Bank of Scotland branch premises at Slamannan, they assaulted the teller, presented a revolver and demanded money from him, placed him in a state of bodily fear and alarm and finally robbed him of £802. The accused denied the charge, and a special defence of an alibi was entered.

MONDAY 16th JUNE 1947

William Penny Thorn, a pig farmer of 12 Holding, The Boggs, Pencaitland, was fined £10 at Haddington Sheriff Court for having slaughtered or caused to be slaughtered for human consumption a pig without a licence granted by or under the authority of the Minister of Food. He was also fined £15 for supplying to a Haddington butcher 160lbs of pork without the authority of a permit issued by or on behalf of the Minister of Food. The butcher, George Anderson of 2 Court Street, Haddington, was fined £30 for obtaining from Thorn 160lbs of pork without authority.

MONDAY 17th JUNE 1929

Weather conditions were favourable for the greyhound fixture at The Powderhall Grounds, Edinburgh, this evening. The attendance was estimated at 8,000. The chief event went to 'Wee Murray', which was the first choice of most backers. It went ahead at the beginning, and running in a dashing, faultless style finished six lengths ahead of its nearest opponent in the good time of 29.60 seconds.

SUNDAY 17th JUNE 1945

An eight-year-old boy, Frederick Jarvie of 3 North St James Street, Edinburgh, was killed when he fell through the glass roof of the Waverley Market in Princes Street. Apparently he had managed to climb up on to the roof from the gardens near the Waverley Market steps. He fell a distance of 30 feet and died instantly. Several witnesses had to be treated for shock after witnessing the tragic spectacle.

WEDNESDAY 18th JUNE 1924

While engaged in the horse haulage of a wagon of coal for shipment at the Western Wharf, Granton, Thomas Stevenson of 23 James Street, Newhaven, had his right foot caught in the points of the rail. Before the wagon could be stopped it had passed over Stevenson's foot, crushing it severely. The left leg was also badly bruised. Stevenson, who was in the employment of the London and North-Eastern Railway Company, was removed to the Edinburgh Royal Infirmary in an ambulance wagon. It was hoped he would not lose a limb as a result of his injuries.

WEDNESDAY 18th JUNE 1947

About an hour after he had been knocked down on the railway line at Granton, Edinburgh, a 76-year-old man, William Wishart, who lived at 12 West Pilton Park, died in Leith Hospital. He was crossing the goods line near West Harbour Road when he was struck by a wagon which was being shunted. Both his legs were amputated but this drastic surgical action did not save his life.

WEDNESDAY 19th JUNE 1566

Queen Mary and her English husband Lord Darnley met just after 9am in the Queen's apartments in the castle, where Darnley grudgingly acknowledged Mary's newborn son James as his own flesh and blood, therefore making the baby the future king of both Scotland and England. He was next in line to the English throne behind his mother, baby James having a strong claim on both sides of his family.

TUESDAY 19th JUNE 1855

The first-ever daily issue of *The Scotsman* hit Edinburgh's news-stands, costing 4d. It had previously been a weekly publication but the repeal of stamp duty allowed for daily publication, and a new name: *The Daily Scotsman*.

TUESDAY 20th JUNE 1933

The Secretary of State for Scotland officially opened a new hospital facility costing £97,000. Situated in Fairmilehead and originally called the Edinburgh Hospital for Crippled Children, when it first opened many of its beds were situated outside, under canvas. The hospital's name would later be judged to be inappropriate and was changed to the Princess Margaret Rose Orthopaedic Hospital, until its closure in 2002.

FRIDAY 21st JUNE 1935

A railway collision that might have had serious consequences, involving the lives of hundreds of children from Yorkshire, occurred this morning at the Waverley Station, Edinburgh. As it was, the children escaped with nothing worse than a fright and a tumble on the floors of the saloon coaches, in which they had travelled to Edinburgh for a day's excursion, and there were no injuries reported beyond a few bumps and bruises.

WEDNESDAY 21st JUNE 1950

Edinburgh Secondary Schools championships at New Meadowbank took place despite heavy rain. Apart from the high jump and the hurdles which were held over until the next day, the programme proceeded without interruption and the standards were again encouragingly high. A record was made by A Gillies (Holy Cross) with a shot-put of 37 ft, but the day's best feat must be credited to another boy from the Ferry Road School, J. Dawson, who equalled the mile record of four minutes and 43.8 seconds despite a sludgy track and heavy rain.

MONDAY 22nd JUNE 1931

About 40 girls employed at a mill at Fountainbridge had an exciting experience in the High Street, Edinburgh. They were proceeding from their work in a Corporation motor bus, and when passing St Giles the engine of the bus suddenly burst into flames. The motor driver at once drew into the side of the road and pulled up, and the girls rushed out. The flames grew to alarming proportions, but the driver, assisted by passing motorists, succeeded in extinguishing them before the arrival of the fire brigade. Fortunately no one was hurt, and the damage to the bus was confined to the engine.

THURSDAY 22nd JUNE 1939

Proposals were put forward for two new Edinburgh cinemas today. Plans were considered at a meeting of the Streets and Buildings Committee in the City Chambers. The Committee considered an application on behalf of Turner Enterprises for approval of the building line of a picture house at Baker's Place, Stockbridge. The other application, for the approval of a building line for the erection of a canopy in Queensferry Road, was on behalf of Associated Cinema Properties Ltd.

TUESDAY 23rd JUNE 1942

Edinburgh received a visit from the leader of the Free French, Charles de Gaulle. The French general gave a rousing speech in which he praised the gallantry of the Scottish soldiers who had forlornly tried to help defend his country from the Nazi invasion of 1940. He also spoke at great length, and in very warm and noble tones, about the 'Auld Alliance'.

WEDNESDAY 23rd JUNE 1954

George Alexander Robertson became the last criminal to be hanged in Edinburgh, following his conviction some four months earlier for a sickening attack on his former wife and their two children at their home in Tron Square. Robertson stabbed his ex-wife Elizabeth and their daughter Jean before following his son, George Jnr, into a neighbour's house where the boy had ran to escape the slaughter. Robertson had stabbed his son in front of the terrified neighbours then dragged the body back to the house in Tron Square and dumped it next to that of his dead mother and badly wounded sister, before trying to gas himself by putting his head into the oven. Police thwarted his suicide attempt and their prompt actions meant that young Jean survived the sickening ordeal after medical treatment.

TUESDAY 24th JUNE 1969

The C&A department store in Princes Street became the first shop in Edinburgh to be fitted with security CCTV. Forty cameras were placed in the shop in an attempt to combat the increase in shoplifting in the capital. The cameras had another handy use for staff as they allowed management to see how busy different departments were at any one time. Edinburgh looked forward to a new era of secure shopping at the facility.

WEDNESDAY 24th JUNE 1998

Readers of *The Scotsman* and the *Evening News* won their battle to save the Princess Alexandra Eye Pavilion. Over 100,000 people supported the campaign led by the papers, staff and patients. Lothian Health Board's chairman Margaret Ford personally intervened to save the unit.

SUNDAY 25th JUNE 1876

An Edinburgh man named Peter Thompson was one of forty or so lucky 7th Cavalry troopers who became separated from Custer's battalion only moments before it was surrounded and wiped out by Sioux and Cheyenne warriors at the Little Bighorn. Thompson claimed to be one of only two living witnesses to the 'last stand' from the American side. Twenty other Scots were not so fortunate, and died with around 265 of their comrades, almost half of the entire regiment.

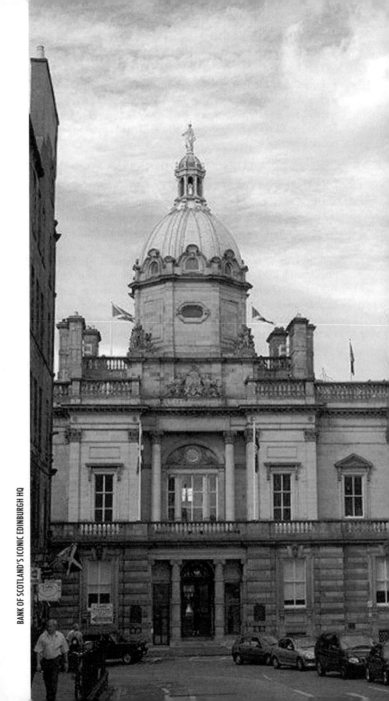

THURSDAY 25th JUNE 1891

Publication of the first Sherlock Holmes story by Edinburgh-born author Arthur Conan Doyle in *The Strand* magazine triggered the start of success for the stories. Earlier publication of 'A Study in Scarlet', in *Beeton's Christmas Annual* in 1887, had attracted very little public interest.

TUESDAY 26th JUNE 1928

John Loch, a 19-year-old postman, pleaded guilty at Edinburgh Sheriff Court to having, on five occasions between January and June, stolen postal packets containing either money or postal orders. An agent on behalf of the accused put forward a plea for leniency on account of his youth. The total amount of money involved, he said, was £3 8s of which 50s had been recovered. Mr Horn, the Fiscal, said Loch had entered the service of the Post Office in 1923, and was employed as a messenger until September last, when he was appointed a postman. One of his duties was to go round collecting letters from pillar boxes, and on the last occasion he stole a letter which had been put in the box. Sentence of three months' imprisonment was passed.

THURSDAY 27th JUNE 1935

It was discovered a hut behind the Cavalry Barracks at Redford in Edinburgh was broken into, and an ammunition box opened. An 18-pounder blank cartridge fitted with primer was missing, and a warning had been issued by the police that the cartridge was highly dangerous if handled by anyone without knowledge and care. Any person who may have information on the matter was asked to communicate with the police or the military authorities.

TUESDAY 27th JUNE 1950

Two members of the Edinburgh City Police – Gerald McDaid and William Hamilton Russell – appeared in Edinburgh Burgh Court charged with seriously assaulting a prisoner while he was in custody. It was alleged the assault took place in Albert Street, Leith, and in a police box there, where it was alleged the officers subjected their victim to a monstrous beating. The accused pleaded not guilty through an agent and trial was fixed for August 3rd.

TUESDAY 28th JUNE 1989

A crowd of 28,553 packed Tynecastle Park to see Scotland take on Portugal in the semi-final of the under 16s World Cup. Hosted in the country, high demand and public interest in the game saw thousands of unlucky fans locked out of the stadium as Scotland beat a Portugal side, containing a young Luis Figo, 1-0, to claim a place in the final against Saudi Arabia.

THURSDAY 28th JUNE 1990

Over 1,500 protestors carrying flags from 40 countries marched through Edinburgh in a bid to save maternity services at the Western General Hospital. The unit was under threat thanks to a £2.4 million cuts and closures package proposed by Lothian Health Board. The marchers made their way from King Stables Road to Old St Andrew's House where they presented a petition to Lord Provost Eleanor McLaughlin.

FRIDAY 29th JUNE 1945

The total amount obtained from the Blood Transfusion Service week in Edinburgh, including house-to-house collections and the Flag Day, was £2,423. Miss Helen White, the organiser for south-east Scotland for the Service, in reporting this result, paid tribute to the work of the district conveners, the numerous collectors who co-operated, and the contributors.

SUNDAY 30th JUNE 1935

An SMT bus and a private car were involved in a head-on collision at New Pentland Garage, near Loanhead, on the main Edinburgh to Penicuik road. The private car was badly smashed and the occupants of the car, a man and a woman, after receiving attention from Dr Hamilton, were taken to Edinburgh Royal Infirmary. The identity of the injured persons was unknown.

SUNDAY 30th JUNE 1946

The King, accompanied by the Queen and by Princess Elizabeth and Princess Margaret, reviewed in Edinburgh a great parade of the British Legion, drawn from all parts of the country. This was held in Scotland's historic parade ground, the King's Park, and was watched by a crowd of 100,000 people.

JULY

TUESDAY 1st JULY 1505

A Royal Seal was granted by Edinburgh Town Council to the Incorporation of Barbers and Surgeons to practise their craft. The organisation is now known as the Royal College of Surgeons of Edinburgh.

THURSDAY 1st JULY 1999

Her Majesty the Queen officially opened the new Scottish Parliament in its temporary home in the Assembly Hall on The Mound, Edinburgh. Sessions would be held there until the new, custom-built Parliament building at Holyrood was completed.

MONDAY 2nd JULY 1990

The campaign to repel Wallace Mercer's hostile takeover bid, which could destroy Hibs and leave Hearts as the only Premier League side in the capital, continued with a rally in the Usher Hall attended by 2,000 football fans. Hearts' leading goalscorer, and self-confessed Hibs fan John Robertson, attended the rally and afterwards he said: "I am here on behalf of the Hearts players who are as determined as anyone else that the Hibs should survive."

SATURDAY 2nd JULY 2005

Around 225,000 protestors descended on Edinburgh for the 'Make Poverty History' march which coincided with the meeting of the G8 at Gleneagles in Fife the following week. The aim of the marchers, who had been told to converge on Edinburgh by Bob Geldof, was to put pressure on the G8 governments to cancel or reduce Third World debt. The marchers heard speeches from political and religious leaders, as well as celebrities who back the cause. They called for the G8 leaders meeting at Gleneagles the following week to take action. The march was one of a number of events planned in the run-up to that Wednesday's G8 summit and was the largest single protest ever held in Scotland.

FRIDAY 3rd JULY 1936

A fascist Blackshirt official was fined £3 at Edinburgh Sheriff Court after being found guilty of a charge of assault at the meeting addressed by Sir Oswald Mosley, the fascist leader, in the Usher Hall, on May 15th.

SUNDAY 3rd JULY 1949

Large crowds thronging the platform joined in the singing of the famous Lourdes hymn 'Bells of the Angelus' as a special train carrying nearly 600 pilgrims to France pulled out of Princes Street Station, Edinburgh. Of the 14 coaches, three marked with a large red cross had been reserved for 64 sick pilgrims and in seven of the carriages were 14 stretcher cases, mostly women. Five white-robed nursing sisters from convents in the city tended to these bed-ridden cases, while mingling with the other sick along the train were two local doctors and two nurses. The last passenger aboard was a young Edinburgh man who was a fighter pilot during the war. Unable to walk or even leave his carriage because of severe spinal injuries sustained in a crash, he had to make the long trip south in the guard's van. The journey to Lourdes was expected to take 33 hours.

SUNDAY 4th JULY 1915

A hospital train arrived in Princes Street station, Edinburgh, from Southampton with a hundred wounded soldiers from the Western Front. The usual arrangements were made by the Red Cross Society for the conveyance of the men, all of whom were local, to hospital.

WEDNESDAY 4th JULY 1934

Over a thousand children from the special schools of Edinburgh were entertained to a picnic at Norton Park, Ratho, through the auspices of the High Constables of Edinburgh and the Courant Fund. The funds were supplied from both of these sources, and both organisations were represented by committees to carry out the arrangements and attend to the sports and needs of the children. The outing was greatly enjoyed, and the weather gloriously warm and sunny. It was hoped the event would be repeated annually.

FRIDAY 5th JULY 1560

The signing of the Treaty of Edinburgh formally brought an end to 'the auld alliance' between Scotland and France. English commissioners, French commanders and the Scots nobility agreed a peace deal that would see all French soldiers sent home, with the exception of two tiny garrisons at Dunbar and Inchkeith, who left later.

FRIDAY 5th JULY 1996

Ian Wilmut and Keith Campbell at the Roslin Research Institute stunned the world by unveiling their latest creation – an artificially cloned female sheep named 'Dolly'. The sheep had been created using a process called somatic cell nuclear transfer, the original stem cells coming from another sheep's mammary gland. She got her name from the link between 'mammaries' and big-breasted country singer Dolly Parton, of whom both Dolly's creators were fans.

WEDNESDAY 6th JULY 1921

Field Marshall Sir William Robertson unveiled two bronze panels inscribed with the names of all the 155 members of the Royal Scots Greys Regiment who were killed during the Great War. The panels were attached to the bottom of the memorial statue in Princes Street Gardens. Thousands of members of the public gathered in the vicinity and the family and loved ones of the fallen were housed on a special platform beneath the statue. Sir William Robertson said that "while they were met to do honour to those who gave their lives in the war, they must also not forget those men who went out and did their duty and returned home broken in health and found it difficult to get work".

MONDAY 6th JULY 2009

A number of monkeys, who escaped after being moved to a new enclosure at Edinburgh Zoo, were still on the loose. The Barbary macaques, which were not said to pose a threat to humans, made their bid for freedom on Friday. Zookeepers with nets were now trying to tempt the monkeys down from trees at the Corstorphine Hill site. A zoo spokeswoman said some of the monkeys had been recaptured, but an undisclosed number were still free within the grounds of the zoo. She said the escape had involved a small number of the Barbary macaques.

FRIDAY 7th JULY 1559

In what was a pivotal year ecclesiastically in Scotland, John Knox became the country's first-ever Protestant Minister after a ceremony in Edinburgh. Scotland was in the midst of great upheaval as disgruntled priests like Knox sought to change the country's religion from Catholicism.

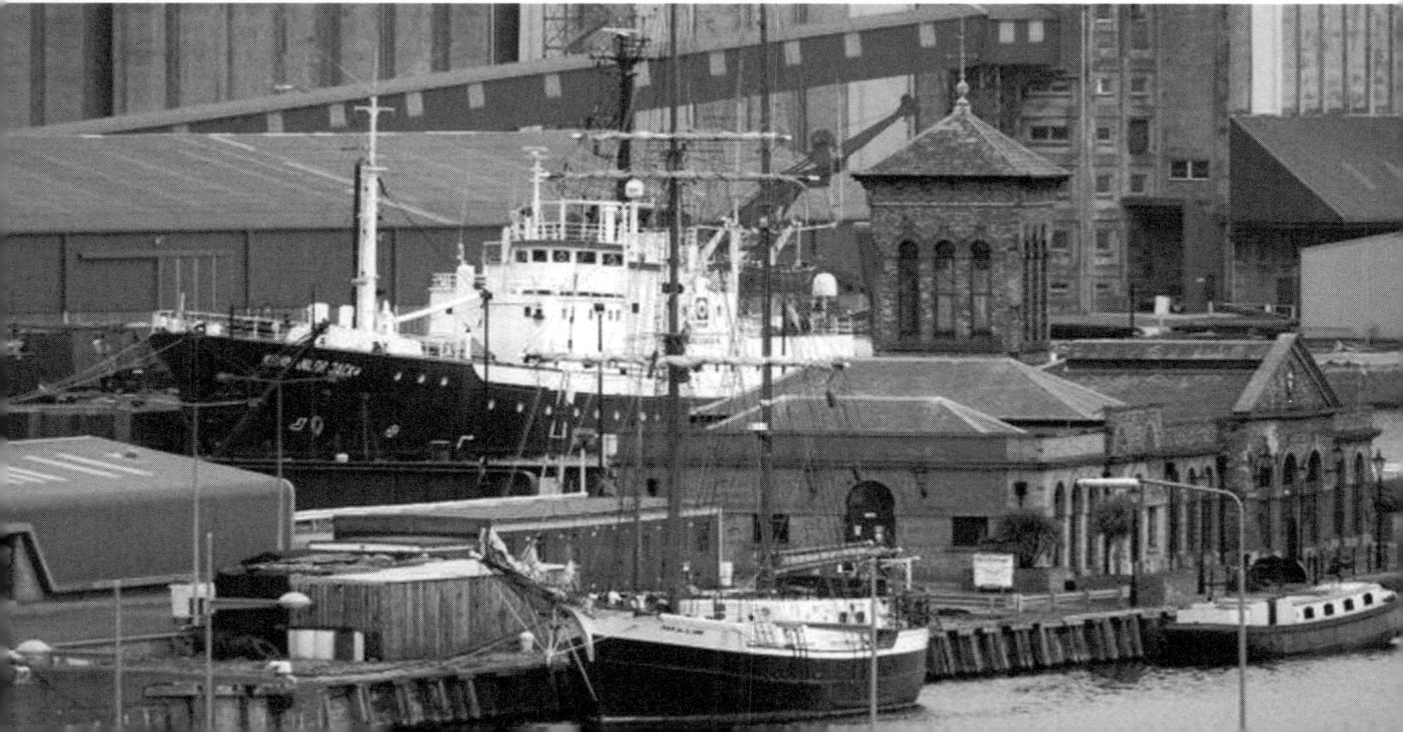

FRIDAY 7th JULY 1978

A royal parade at Holyrood Park opened with a 21-gun salute from a battery on Arthur's Seat but nearly ended in farce when Warrant Officer Peter Haynes backed his horse, Sea King, into a rank of dismounted troopers after the animal reared up in panic at the Royal Salute. The timely intervention of another trooper allowed Haynes to regain control of his mount, though Haynes never once dropped the regimental colours that he and Sea King were bearing for the parade, which was held in celebration of the 300th 'birthday' of the Royal Scots Dragoon Guards.

MONDAY 8th JULY 1918

The King and Queen of the Belgians, visiting this country in connection with the Royal silver wedding celebrations, travelled from London to Edinburgh and took up residence at the North British Station Hotel. Commander Sir Charles Cust, Equerry to the King, was in attendance upon their majesties, and other members of the suite were Brigadier General the Earl of Athlone and Major A Gordon. The visit was of a purely private nature. In the morning, their majesties visited the castle and other points of interest in the Royal Mile, and the afternoon was spent on a visit to Rosyth Dockyard.

TUESDAY 8th JULY 1941

The death occurred in the Edinburgh Royal Hospital for Sick Children of a one-and-a-half-year-old child, Thelma McIllroy, as a result of scalding injuries received the previous Friday. At her home in the dwelling house of London Road Fire Station, she upset a bowl of hot water.

MONDAY 9th JULY 1923

A train travelling from Aberdeen to Edinburgh carrying tons of fresh fish and meat was derailed between Newington and Blackford stations, blocking the line and causing mayhem as detritus was scattered all over the area and around the track, much to the delight of local wildlife. The locomotive had been diverted from its usual more direct route into the capital. Remarkably, no-one was killed or seriously injured, despite the carriages overturning. The guard, a Dundee man, had the luckiest escape and was extremely shaken.

TUESDAY 9th JULY 1935

Sentence of three months' imprisonment was passed by Sheriff-Principal Brown at Edinburgh Sheriff Court on Henry Miller, who admitted having contracted a 'bigamous marriage' with a Leith woman in Edinburgh on October 26th, 1934. It was stated that Miller had been married in 1900, and there were two grown-up children from the union. He had been parted from his legal wife since 1903.

SUNDAY 10th JULY 1633

The sailing ship *Blessing of Burntisland*, carrying gold, jewellery, silver plate and other treasures belonging to King Charles I, sank in rough conditions in the Firth of Forth. Its skipper had initially voiced concerns about impending bad weather, but his concerns were ignored by royal aides who were more preoccupied with moving the King's treasure.

MONDAY 10th JULY 1944

Following a broadcast radio SOS, the parents of a year-old baby boy took the child back to Leith Hospital. The mother had taken him to the hospital for an X-ray at a rush period on Sunday. His name was recorded, but the address of the parents was not taken, and the broadcast stated that the X-ray showed it was urgent the baby should return. He was detained in hospital.

WEDNESDAY 11th JULY 1923

King George V took time out from the affairs of state to visit Edinburgh and open the first section of the new state-of-the-art power station at Portobello. He took time out to meet a hand-picked group of local children.

WEDNESDAY 11th JULY 1934

Shortly after two o'clock in the morning, in a dense haze, the steam trawler *Taldos of Granton* became stranded on the rocks at the South Carr, on the East Lothian coast. The vessel was driven well on to the rocks through the force of the impact. Dunbar motor lifeboat was called out, and during the day stood by the vessel. The trawler was re-floated that afternoon and taken in tow to Leith by a tug-boat.

SATURDAY 12th JULY 1698

The Darien Expedition left Leith heading for Panama, where the Scots hoped to establish a trading post in the New World that would revitalise Scotland's economy and make her a world-power, if it succeeded. Led by William Paterson, thousands of ordinary Scottish folk invested money in the expedition, to the tune of approximately £500,000, about half of the national capital available. Almost every Scot who had £5 to spare invested in the Darien scheme. Thousands more volunteered to travel on board the five chartered ships hired to carry the pioneers to their new home where Scots could settle, including famine-driven Highlanders and soldiers discharged following the Glencoe Massacre.

THURSDAY 12th JULY 1945

An eight-year-old girl named Phyllis Merritt, whose parents resided at 6 St James' Place, Edinburgh, was found dead shortly after three o'clock in an air-raid shelter situated between St John's Hill and Holyrood Road, Edinburgh. She had received severe head injuries. A young man was taken into custody by the police and would appear the next morning at the Burgh Court.

FRIDAY 13th JULY 2007

A new trial hovercraft crossing of the Firth of Forth was officially launched. The Stagecoach service between Kirkcaldy in Fife and Portobello in Edinburgh would carry up to 130 passengers at a time, starting from Monday July 16th. Officially launching the two-week trial, Transport Minister Stewart Stevenson said: "This is an innovative trial which has the potential to change the way people travel between Fife and Edinburgh. If we are to tackle congestion on Scotland's roads and encourage people out of their cars, we must give people a wide range of public transport choices. This trial gives people that added choice. I hope as many people as possible take advantage of the hovercraft service and make this trial a success." The £300,000 trial was part-funded by the South East of Scotland Transport Partnership (SEStran). It would offer a 20-minute crossing time, using a 28-metre BHT130 hovercraft, incorporating the latest diesel engine technology. A total of 22 services a day – 11 in each direction – would operate on the route, with peak-time services and integrated bus links.

SATURDAY 14th JULY 1798

Following on from recently winning her independence from Britain, the fledgling government of the United States of America opened its first consulate in Edinburgh.

THURSDAY 14th JULY 1927

Thousands turned out to witness the opening of the Scottish National War Memorial at Edinburgh Castle. The structure commemorated those Scots killed in British service up to 1918 and was an impressive sight that was expected to attract thousands more in the coming months.

MONDAY 15th JULY 1889

Edinburgh received a major cultural boost with the opening of The National Portrait Gallery for Scotland, in the city's Queen Street.

SUNDAY 15th JULY 1923

The kind and generous interest of Sir Robert and Lady Maule in the cripples of the city was again demonstrated when 200 crippled children and adults spent a happy time at their residence, Ashbrook, Ferry Road, Edinburgh. After tea, the guests were entertained by a company of minstrels. Each guest, upon leaving, received a large bunch of flowers, a bag of fruit and a useful toy or gift.

MONDAY 16th JULY 1928

A tragic discovery was made in a house at 7 Bothwell Street, Edinburgh, when James Petrie Stott, a taxi driver, was found dead in his bed. The blankets were over his head and a gas tube, attached to a bunsen, was found to be underneath them. Stott, who was 47 years of age, had sent his daughter to buy something for dinner. When she returned, after being half an hour away, she found the door barred by two chairs placed behind it.

THURSDAY 16th JULY 1970

The Duke of Edinburgh opened the ninth Commonwealth Games at Meadowbank Stadium amid the backdrop of a 21-gun salute and a fly-past by three RAF squadrons. A crowd of 30,000 spectators attended the ceremony, which heralded the start of the games featuring 1,700 athletes from 42 different countries.

TUESDAY 17th JULY 1537

Lady Jane Douglas was burned at the stake for witchcraft and treason by King James V after a jealous noble had fabricated evidence and extracted statements from Lady Jane's family. Lady Glamis, as she was also known, was now thought to haunt Glamis Castle, some 60 miles north of Edinburgh, where she was known as 'The Grey Lady'.

SUNDAY 17th JULY 1695

A new financial institution, the Bank of Scotland, was established. It was the first bank to be established by an Act of the Scottish Parliament.

THURSDAY 18th JULY 1940

A small number of people became Edinburgh's first civilian casualties of the war after a Luftwaffe raid on the capital. One 18-year-old victim from Leith died because she had taken refuge in an air-raid shelter.

TUESDAY 18th JULY 1950

Following a fight in a public house at 85 High Riggs, Edinburgh on Monday night, Edinburgh Police were called and found a barman, Peter Allan Fernie of 41 Oxgangs Terrace, seriously injured. He was taken to the Royal Infirmary where he died later. In connection with the affair, another barman, James McGill of 4 Springvalley Terrace, appeared at Edinburgh Court charged with murder. No plea was taken. McGill was remanded in custody until July 25th.

FRIDAY 19th JULY 1644

After being imprisoned in a small hole normally reserved for adulterers for a time, Sir John Gordon of Haddo, who had been second in command of the Royalist Forces in Scotland during the War of the Three Kingdoms, was executed for treason at the Mercat Cross.

THURSDAY 19th JULY 1919

Edinburgh was awash with cheering crowds and adorned with flags and banners as the city celebrated Victory Day with a huge parade. Thousands turned out to see Scottish Regiments, along with their horses, tanks and armoured cars, parade through the city to rapturous applause.

THURSDAY 20th JULY 1922

Whilst cycling along the Queensferry Road at Barnton, Thomas Whyte, aged 13, whose parents lived at 15 Barclay Place, Edinburgh, collided with a motor bus. He had been riding in front of the bus when he suddenly turned without giving warning, the heavy vehicle throwing him from his flimsy machine. He was taken to the Royal Infirmary, and died of his injuries shortly after admission.

MONDAY 20th JULY 1942

The baby orang-utan which was born at Edinburgh Zoo a week ago, died today. The first of its species ever to be born in captivity in this country, the arrival aroused considerable interest at the Scottish Zoo, and attracted large numbers of visitors to the enclosure. It was stated the offspring of Mickey and Minnie, two of the most treasured specimens in the zoo, was known from the outset not to be a 'strong baby'.

THURSDAY 21st JULY 1927

At a press interview in Glasgow, Sir Harry Lauder of 'Roamin' in the Gloamin' fame was asked what he thought about Edinburgh's decision to award him the freedom of the city. He answered: "It is very nice of them. My father was from the capital and I am of course originally from Portobello, so it was a nice, kind thought that I appreciate greatly." Mr Lauder then went to a nursing home to visit his sick wife.

FRIDAY 21st JULY 1933

A number of Edinburgh town councillors viewed the scene of their municipal responsibility from the top of a high tower. The point of view, in actual fact, was about 240 feet from the ground. The party were inspecting the new water gas plant at Granton Gas Works, and in the course of their visit they went up to the top of the new gasometer, which in appearance resembled a Chinese pagoda. This large and massive tower was surrounded by five successive galleries connected with outside stairways, but the party went up in the lift, which took fully two minutes from the ground to the top of the shaft. A slanting passage led on to the convex summit of the tower.

FRIDAY 22nd JULY 1913

A new zoological park, Edinburgh Zoo, opened its doors for the first time, in the city's Corstorphine Hill area.

TUESDAY 22nd JULY 1975

The reason for the existence of the £100,000 pedestrian flyover spanning Leith Street was finally explained by Alex Crockett, Director of Highways for Lothian Region. The reason the bridge was built was to link the giant shopping complex with a nearby housing scheme, which has since been abandoned. Crockett defended the structure, pointing out it is still useful for providing a link between St Andrew's House and the New St Andrew's House. Councillor Wilson, in stark contrast, had described the bridge as an 'absolute monstrosity'.

THURSDAY 23rd JULY 1925

The Parks Committee of Edinburgh Town Council, after over an hour's discussion, decided, by nine votes to two, to recommend the use of the Meadows be granted to the Highland and Agricultural Society for their annual show in 1927. The principal reason behind the decision was because trade in the city would benefit considerably. Those who opposed the grant made representations on behalf of the cricketers using the Meadows during the summer months. It was stated that if the Meadows was utilised as a showground, the cricketers would be unable to make use of their pitches for a considerable time.

THURSDAY 24th JULY 1958

Notorious serial killer Peter Manuel was the subject of vigorous security measures as his appeal against his conviction for seven murders was heard at Parliament House. Lawyers decided Manuel should remain in the holding cell, rather than appear in the court itself, as an angry mob waited outside. His appeal failed and he was hanged at Barlinnie Prison in Glasgow. Among his seven victims had been a couple and their ten-year-old son.

MONDAY 24th JULY 1967

British Rail announced St Margaret's locomotive yard near Jock's Lodge would close on August 7th, with stock being transferred to Millerhill, Leith Central and Haymarket.

THURSDAY 24th JULY 1986

Despite running into financial difficulties and being boycotted by 'black' nations over Margaret Thatcher's Government's support of pro-apartheid South Africa, Edinburgh put on a magnificent opening ceremony for the Commonwealth Games, with 6,500 tartan-clad schoolchildren participating all the way from the castle esplanade to Meadowbank Stadium, where they danced and sang along to 'spirit of youth', the games' anthem. Bermuda's team participated in the ceremony, but were ordered to leave and join the boycott immediately after.

TUESDAY 25th JULY 1933

A total of 77 police officers, led by Sergeant William Merrilees, raided the Kosmo Club in Swinton Row, off Leith Street, in a bid to end a call girl racket being run by the club's owner, Asher Barnard. The venue, which had been operating under the cloak of being a 'dance club', was stormed by the police, much to the consternation of the 150 patrons present and that of Barnard, who was jailed for 18 months for living off immoral earnings. Merrilees had been offered bribes to turn a blind eye to goings on at the Kosmo, but had treated the offers, three of which were for brand-new cars, with disdain.

THURSDAY 25th JULY 1946

The body of Miss Grace Wilson of 64 Lorne Street, Leith, who was employed as manageress of an Edinburgh loan office, was found in the woods at Dunsappie Loch, King's Park, Edinburgh. Unsuccessful dredging operations followed the discovery of a woman's handbag at the lochside on Tuesday. A Holyrood Park worker discovered the body, and the police were notified. It was taken to the City Mortuary, where it was later identified as being that of Miss Wilson, who had been missing since July 16th.

THURSDAY 26th JULY 1923

The international lawn tennis match between Scotland and England was resumed at Murrayfield, Edinburgh, in conjunction with the Scottish National Championships meeting. On Wednesday, each country had scored a point, and today Scotland scored two points to England's one. Final combined result was Scotland 3 England 2, between doubles and singles.

FRIDAY 26th JULY 1940

The General Purposes Committee of Edinburgh Town Council decided to take down iron railings in Nicolson and St Patrick squares, and also in the Meadows, Bruntsfield Links, Relugas Road and Inverleith Park, so the iron could be utilised by government industry to aid the war effort.

SUNDAY 27th JULY 1760

The Scottish School of Design was founded in Edinburgh. It later became the Royal Institution, and finally the Royal Scottish Academy.

THURSDAY 27th JULY 1950

Sheriff James Macdonald addressed two tearful 13-year-old Leith girls at Edinburgh Sheriff Juvenile Court and told them they did not seem to realise how serious it was to give a false message to the fire brigade. The girls had admitted giving a false fire alarm, by means of a 999 call, from a kiosk in Leith Walk.

MONDAY 28th JULY 1913

Tram drivers were injured and two protestors were arrested amid ugly scenes as the Edinburgh tram strike continued. Thirty-five cars were 'out', an increase of five on the previous day, and they were crowded with passengers. That this day-to-day increase of cars was having an unfortunate effect on the temper of the men was shown by outbreaks of disorder. For their participation in these offences one striker was arrested for assault, and another for breach of the peace. The most serious incident of the day was a brutal attack made on three tramway servants in Iona Street by an excited mob of strikers and others, in the course of which two of the workers were seriously injured. The force of police at Shrubhill had to be considerably increased as a result.

MONDAY 28th JULY 2003

Lothian and Borders Police made a gruesome discovery following an anonymous tip-off. A man's remains were found in a suitcase where the Water of Leith flows into Leith Docks. Police said they believed they knew the identity of the victim and were 'following a definite line of inquiry'.

WEDNESDAY 29th JULY 1925

A young woman, who was found wandering Princes Street babbling incoherent nonsense on Monday night, apparently suffering from some sort of amnesia or memory loss, regained her memory but was detained until the next day at Edinburgh Royal Infirmary, pending further examination.

MONDAY 29th JULY 1929

The death took place in Leith Hospital of William Cockburn of 35 Claremont Gardens, Leith, as the result of him falling into the water at Leith Docks that Sunday afternoon. Cockburn was walking along the quay of the Edinburgh Dock when he accidentally fell into the water. Two seamen dived to his aid from vessels in the vicinity, and kept him afloat till assistance arrived. Cockburn was removed to Leith Hospital, but never recovered from the shock of his immersion.

SATURDAY 30th JULY 1335

The Battle of Burgh-Muir was fought just outside Edinburgh, between 200 Men-at-Arms and Archers allied to England under the Count of Namur and local Scottish forces under the Earl of Moray. Caught in the open on the Burgh Muir, the English troops were chased all the way to Edinburgh Castle by the Scots. The castle's defences had been slighted though, and the English were forced to kill their own horses to plug breaches in the walls. They put up a fight until more Scottish troops arrived, compelling them to seek terms from the Scots. Namur was released and escorted back to England. When Scottish troops stripped the English bodies of their armour, they found out one of their opponents – who had fought tenaciously – had actually been a woman in disguise.

SATURDAY 30th JULY 1994

Rezerection's 'The Event 2' rave was held outdoors at the Royal Highland Showground. This proved to be bigger and better organised than 'The Event', with an attendance of around 16,000 hardcore ravers from all over the UK and beyond. The line-up also had a global feel to it as local talent such as Bass-X and The Rhythmic State were joined by established international artists like Lenny Dee, Carl Cox, Laurent Garnier and Human Resource.

WEDNESDAY 31st JULY 1946

A young soldier was admonished by Sheriff Macdonald when he appeared before him at Edinburgh Sheriff Court on a charge arising out of a shooting accident in which a girl was injured. The soldier, Lance Corporal Allan Ralph Wragg of Redford Barracks, pleaded guilty to having had in his possession a .22 revolver and 382 rounds of ammunition without being the holder of a firearms certificate, contrary to the Firearms Act of 1937. Mr J Gray, Depute Procurator-Fiscal, said that on July 11th, a 17-year-old girl was admitted to a city hospital suffering from a gunshot wound on the leg. It transpired that Wragg had been sitting with the girl on a seat in a park. He had been showing her how a revolver worked and, unfortunately, it had gone off accidentally.

AUGUST

THURSDAY 1st AUGUST 1907

A trial got underway in Edinburgh that, if successful, would hopefully reduce the number of traffic accidents in the capital. Illuminated signs were fitted to the city's tramcars, the same type currently in use in Glasgow. The letters were in white on a black background and a special gas was the magic ingredient used to illuminate them. In contrast, only one motor vehicle in Edinburgh had a similar sign. It was hoped the scheme would drastically reduce the number of accidents in the capital.

MONDAY 1st AUGUST 1949

Frank Nash of 24 Polwarth Gardens, Edinburgh, received multiple injuries and suffered from concussion when a motor car which he was driving in Leith Walk collided with a tram island at Pilrig. The car was badly damaged. Nash, who was the only occupant of the car, was removed to the Royal Infirmary, and his condition that evening was described as 'serious'. This was the latest in a long run of recent accidents involving cars and trams.

WEDNESDAY 2nd AUGUST 1922

One of Edinburgh's most famous sons, Alexander Graham Bell, died in Cape Breton Island, Nova Scotia. He invented the telephone and was also renowned for his work with the deaf.

THURSDAY 2nd AUGUST 1934

A Norwegian naval flotilla, consisting of a minelayer, three torpedo boats, and three submarines, arrived early in Leith Roads. In the evening, they entered the docks and were berthed there, along with submarines in the Imperial Dock, and the other vessels in the Edinburgh Dock. On leaving Leith they would proceed to Stavangar. Although it was not until seven o'clock that evening the vessels entered the docks, such was the interest, crowds of hundreds of people visited at the quayside. As the flotilla had approached Leith that morning, they fired a salute, which was returned from Edinburgh Castle's Half-Moon Battery.

MONDAY 3rd AUGUST 1573

Sir William Kirkcaldy of Grange was executed for treason, after heroically defending Edinburgh Castle on behalf of Mary Queen of Scots from May 17th to May 28th 1573.

MONDAY 3rd AUGUST 1932

The opening of the 'Tanks for Attack' campaign in Edinburgh coincided with a Bank Holiday, but the organisers were aiming less at daily spurts than a sustained effort over a period of ten weeks. The banks were co-operating as usual but in contrast to Warships Week, attention was being concentrated mainly on the small saver and much of the campaigning would be done by street savings group collectors. The target figure was £1,250,000, representing the sum necessary for 25 tanks, and the city and the various wards would have their names inscribed on the battle tanks towards which they had contributed.

WEDNESDAY 4th AUGUST 1909

A near-hysterical *Evening News* reported that the western part of Princes Street Gardens had been taken over by vagrants and drunks, who 'sprawled in ungainly attitudes' next to the Ross Fountain and on the slopes of the castle. The paper called for action by the Parks Committee.

TUESDAY 5th AUGUST 1704

The Act of Security was passed by the Scottish Parliament. This allowed Scotland to choose a successor to Queen Anne other than the one elected by the English Parliament, if Scottish conditions were not met. Many Scots favoured inviting the son of the exiled King James to come home and be king of his ancestral kingdom. This precipitated the demands in London for an Act of Union of the two parliaments.

FRIDAY 5th AUGUST 1927

The Edinburgh District Branch of the Overseas League – the first Scottish branch of that body – was formally opened at 2 North Charlotte Street by the Earl of Cassillis. The league's headquarters were in London, and there was a branch in Liverpool, and a number in the Dominions. The Edinburgh premises were situated on two floors at the address mentioned above, and included a comfortably furnished lounge and reading rooms for ladies and gentlemen. They were opened to members of the league about three weeks beforehand, and had already been visited by large numbers of people from overseas places like America, Canada, Australia, New Zealand, South Africa, and many other parts of the world. The league was a non-party British society; its object was the promotion of the unity of British subjects.

SATURDAY 6th AUGUST 1678

The first Glasgow to Edinburgh coach service began from the White Horse Inn, Edinburgh.

MONDAY 6th AUGUST 1934

A mountaineering feline caused pandemonium when it climbed some 50 feet up the Castle Rock then became stranded, unable to either ascend or descend to safety. Its cries for help attracted people and a policeman was soon on the scene. The kitten was eventually rescued by the fire brigade, who then placed the animal in the care of the police.

WEDNESDAY 6th AUGUST 1941

Two people were killed and four wounded in a final German air-assault on the capital, with the bombs exploding in Craigentinny, bringing Edinburgh's casualty toll from air raids during the war to 20 deaths and 210 serious injuries.

SATURDAY 7th AUGUST 1734

Major Griffiths, Edinburgh Castle's commander, was drowned with all of his party whilst fishing in the Firth of Forth. The night before, his wife had dreamed neither her husband nor his companions would return from the fishing trip, and she had begged them not to go in case they drowned. Her concerns had been ignored.

WEDNESDAY 7th AUGUST 1935

Kapitanleutnant Ernst Gruber, commandant of the German cruiser Elbe lying docked at Leith, visited the Edinburgh City Chambers to pay a courtesy call on the authorities. He greeted Baillie Raithby, who received him with a Nazi salute. The meeting took place in the Lord Provost's room. Kapitanleutnant Gruber was accompanied by the German Consul in Edinburgh, Mr A Dacker.

FRIDAY 8th AUGUST 1930

At today's sitting of Edinburgh Dean of Guild Court, warrant was granted for the erection, by the Corporation, of 204 houses at Slateford Road and Moat Street. The houses would be built in blocks of six or more, and would each consist of three apartments; living room and two bedrooms, with scullery and bathroom.

THURSDAY 8th AUGUST 1986

Two 11-year-old boys were ordered to be detained in a remand home for three weeks, and sentence was deferred for six months in the case of a younger boy at a Juvenile Court in Edinburgh. The case was a sequel to vandalism which resulted in a school being closed to pupils for an entire day. The boys, pupils of a well-known fee-paying school, damaged articles at Blackhall Public School and in its outlying buildings.

THURSDAY 9th AUGUST 1934

The day before the historic Ferry Fair at South Queensferry, the town was paraded by the Burry Man. In accordance with a local tradition, the origins of which are now sadly lost to antiquity, local man Alexander Sinclair acted the historic part, being covered in thousands of Burdock plant heads, to the point he was unable to see and needed assistance to walk from house to house. The local area had earlier been scoured to find enough of these 'burrs'.

SATURDAY 9th AUGUST 1986

Rangers' expensively assembled squad under new player-manager Graeme Souness faced an opening-day trip to Easter Road. The home side won the match 2-1 with goals from Stuart Beedie and Steve Cowan, Ally McCoist netting the Gers goal from the penalty spot, but the result was overshadowed by extraordinary events that occurred on the pitch in between play. Souness was sent off for a disgusting, very deliberate tackle on Hibs' George McCluskey which broke the veteran forward's leg. As a result of the challenge, a mass brawl between the opposing teams took place on the pitch, with every single player being booked apart from Hibs' keeper Alan Rough, who was the only player who avoided the 'stramash' and thus received no yellow card.

TUESDAY 10th AUGUST 1915

It was reported at a meeting of Edinburgh Territorial Force Association that during the three weeks ending last week, over 580 recruits were obtained for the Territorial units of the city. Satisfaction was expressed by all present with the steady rate of enlistment. Many of those who had enlisted already had previous military experience and firearms training, and it was hoped this extra military know-how would further boost the morale of the troops at the front, civil defence forces and the local populace.

TUESDAY 10th AUGUST 1928

Amid still-tight fuel rationing, William Brown Crawford, a bank clerk from 29 Dryden Gardens, Edinburgh, was alleged to have motored to Caithness with petrol grafted for driving his invalid mother, and taking his young son to and from school. He was fined £10 at Edinburgh Sheriff Court for misusing the petrol. The Ministry of Fuel and Power had received information that Crawford had made the journey, and his application form was examined. Crawford said he had 'saved the petrol up'.

SUNDAY 11th AUGUST 2002

The first Edinburgh derby of the season at Tynecastle saw Jambos' Dutch striker Mark De Vries score four of Hearts' five goals in their 5-1 victory. Andy Kirk opened the scoring in the first half, while Ian Murray netted what turned out to be Hibs' consolation just after the break. The scoreline flattered Hearts. Hibs endured a late defensive collapse, but the Jambos deserved their victory nonetheless. It was an afternoon to forget for hapless Hibs keeper Tony Caig, who was to blame for two goals.

WEDNESDAY 12th AUGUST 1936

Fire broke out on the top floor of the Old Waverley Hotel, Princes Street, Edinburgh. Fortunately, the outbreak, although it caused a good deal of excitement on the street below, was speedily extinguished by the fire brigade. Two bedrooms were destroyed, but two hundred guests staying in the hotel were practically undisturbed and did not leave the building while the brigade were at work, some even opting to sleep through the excitement.

THURSDAY 12th AUGUST 1948

Francis Ryan of 407 Longmore Street in Glasgow and James Fairweather of no fixed residence, were sent to prison for 60 days at Edinburgh Burgh court when they were found guilty of being known thieves found frequenting Gorgie Road, Edinburgh, on the last Saturday with intent to commit theft. Mr JD Heatly the City Prosecutor said that Ryan's Court appearances went back to before the start of the century. Fairweather had ten previous court appearances, and both accused had been convicted at Glasgow Police Court for a similar offence.

SATURDAY 13th AUGUST 1921

The *Edinburgh Evening News* reported that the Scottish Amateur Athletic season, which was about to end, had been a remarkable one. In particular, one Eric H Liddell had had an extraordinary summer, running the 100 yards in 10.25 seconds at one meet. At just 19-years-old, Liddell has proved himself to be the finest sprinter since A R Downer. The 1981 film *Chariots of Fire* chronicles and contrasts the lives and viewpoints of Liddell and Harold Abrahams. Liddell was born in China, to Scottish missionary parents.

MONDAY 13th AUGUST 1928

After being convicted of slitting his wife's throat at their home in Pirniefield Place, murderer Allan Wales became the first man to be hanged in Edinburgh's new prison at Saughton.

TUESDAY 14th AUGUST 1827

The foundation stone was laid for George IV Bridge in Edinburgh. The structure itself was not to be completed until 1836 due to lack of funds.

TUESDAY 14th AUGUST 1928

The body of a young man was found at the water's edge on the east side of Granton breakwater, and was removed to the city mortuary. It was identified as the body of Jerome Charles Duncan, a divinity student, 22 years of age, who resided at 31 East London Street, Edinburgh.

SATURDAY 15th AUGUST 1822

King George IV visited Edinburgh, wearing Italian-designed Highland dress with tartan trousers – the first visit to Scotland by the House of Hanover since they had been installed in 1714. Sir Walter Scott was behind the trip, which was the first visit to Scotland by a Hanoverian monarch following years of security fears amid Jacobite plots.

WEDNESDAY 15th AUGUST 1840

The Walter Scott Monument had its foundation stone laid in Princes Street Gardens, honouring the man who had both captured the nation's imagination with his writing and rediscovered the 'lost' Scottish Royal Regalia.

SUNDAY 16th AUGUST 1914

Anxious for news regarding the outbreak of war, thousands of Edinburgh's townsfolk queued at the General Post Office to read the following bulletin: *'German plan of invading France seriously delayed by resistance of Liege and intervention of French cavalry, and consequently French have carried out mobilisation and concentration without hindrance. Various minor Belgian and French successes. German crews to quit the German vessels Goebea and Breslau at Constantinople. No British casualties.'*

FRIDAY 16th AUGUST 1929

Councillor Poole gave his decision at Edinburgh Police Court in a case against Patrick Crossan of 13 Pitt Street. The ex-Heart of Midlothian football player was charged with having been found in Princes Street under the influence of drink while in charge of a motor-car. Crossan pleaded not guilty. Councillor Poole found the charge proven, and imposed a fine of £2, with the option of 20 days' imprisonment.

SATURDAY 17th AUGUST 1560

The Scottish Parliament met in Edinburgh and passed two major pieces of legislation that were to change Scotland forever at what was known as 'The Reformation Parliament'. Essentially anti-Catholic, the Papal Jurisdiction Act and the Confession of Faith Ratification Act banned all Scots from, among other things, becoming Pope. They also declared the Pope had no authority in Scotland.

SATURDAY 17th AUGUST 1996

Corries singer Ronnie Browne sang 'Flower of Scotland' at Murrayfield in front of around 40,000 fans before a fundraising match against Barbarians for the Dunblane Fund, the first time the song had been sung at a Scotland rugby match. The 58-year-old singer's former partner wrote the song, but had died from a brain tumour in 1990.

MONDAY 18th AUGUST 1919

Up until this evening no trace had been found of a boating party of pleasure seekers which left Portobello on Sunday evening, comprised of three Jewish young men. All the boats got back after experiencing difficulty, except the missing one which was swept eastward some miles until it was sighted by an incoming French schooner, which drew alongside and threw a rope.

TUESDAY 19th AUGUST 1561

Mary Queen of Scots landed at Leith on her return from France following the death of her husband, King Francis II, unprepared for the religious fervour that had gripped the country in her absence.

SATURDAY 19th AUGUST 1989

Stunning displays by midfield maestro John Collins, and goalkeeper Andy Goram, gave Hibs a well-deserved victory over champions Rangers at Easter Road. Second-half goals from Keith Houchen and fans' favourite Mickey Weir gave Hibs the win, the latter goal coming after an almost comical mistake by Rangers goalie Bonni Ginzburg.

SUNDAY 20th AUGUST 1944

An ambulance train brought 120 children to the Waverley Station, Edinburgh on their way to the Princess Margaret Rose Hospital. The children were evacuated from hospitals in the London area, and nurses of the Royal National Orthopaedic Hospital travelled with their young patients on the train, and were to remain with them in Edinburgh. The children's ages ranged up to 16 and the patients took a lively interest in the surroundings as they were carried off the train to the waiting Red Cross ambulances. Toys, books and magazines were among the personal effects on the stretchers and wheeled trolleys. One or two boys were seen to have Scout equipment on their stretchers.

SUNDAY 20th AUGUST 1967

Portobello swimming baths re-opened after an 18-month refurbishment that cost around £48,000. Leith Victoria Baths were expected to be given a facelift next.

FRIDAY 21st AUGUST 1925

The occupants of a carriage in a train going from Arbroath to Edinburgh had an alarming experience. As the locomotive reached the Forth Bridge, two sounds resembling gunfire were heard by passengers. In fact, a large stone had been thrown at the carriage, smashing its skylight and sending broken glass and debris flying into it. Though none of the eight adult passengers were injured, a small boy narrowly escaped being beheaded by about a foot. The identity of the stone-thrower, and his motive for doing so, was yet to be established.

WEDNESDAY 21st AUGUST 1946

Edinburgh was strangely silent this lunchtime as a well-known sound was absent from the air. For the third consecutive day, the one o'clock gun failed to fire at its usual time. Sources at the castle blamed a faulty hydraulic mechanism for the failure, and announced plans to 'have the artillery piece serviced tomorrow', and a new firing pin inserted into the breach mechanism.

FRIDAY 22nd AUGUST 1913

Two criminal fire-raising outrages, which police believed to have been the work of militant suffragettes, were discovered early in the northern and southern suburbs of Edinburgh. In the one case an attempt had been made to set fire to Fettes College and the other an attempt was made to fire a villa in Grange Loan. Fortunately, the fires were discovered in time to prevent substantial damage. In the case of the Grange Loan house, suffragette literature and other articles were left to show the origin of the fire-raising and to suggest that women were behind it, and traces of suffragette presence were also discovered at Fettes.

SUNDAY 23rd AUGUST 1931

An attempt to cross the Firth of Forth in a glider formed part of the programme at a display organised by Edinburgh Gliding Club, and held at Silverknowes, Davidson's Mains. The attempt was made by Dr Lowe Wylde, who had given displays to an Edinburgh crowd before, and while it was successful, it gave the large crowd an opportunity of witnessing a new kind of air thrill in the form of aeroplane-towed gliding. Hitherto, gliding displays in Edinburgh had been of the ordinary catapult or auto-towed varieties.

MONDAY 24th AUGUST 1925

The Queen, who was staying at Carberry Tower as the guest of Lord and Lady Elphinstone, spent the greater part of a day at Holyrood Palace, examining the alterations which had been made in the furnishings. She also made a shopping expedition to the High Street in search of antique treasures, and made a number of purchases. Among them were several Oriental-style vases, emblazoned with pagodas.

NEWHAVEN HARBOUR

MONDAY 24th AUGUST 1942

A three-month experimental patrol by civilians for the benefit of schoolchildren was introduced to coincide with the reopening of Edinburgh schools. The new scheme would be operated at dangerous street crossings in the vicinity of schools by some 24 persons, known as Civilian Guides, who had taken over the duty from police, as the latter, on account of manpower shortages, were no longer able to staff all the points, though the most important of these would still be under police control. The guides were predominantly disabled soldiers, but there were a few women who had boards for halting traffic when children were crossing the road. The guides would not have the authority of the police, but it was hoped drivers would obey their signals.

SATURDAY 25th AUGUST 1650

Oliver Cromwell's attempt to circumvent General Leslie's great earthwork that defended Edinburgh came to a halt at Gorgie, where a number of Scottish troops aided by local townsfolk saw off Cromwell's advance guard, thus dissuading Cromwell from further attempts to enter the city while the Scots' army was still intact.

MONDAY 25th AUGUST 1930

Sean Connery was born to Scots-Irish parents in the city's Fountainbridge area. A milkman in Tollcross, he went on to become an actor, after refusing a contract to play for Manchester United. Probably most famous for his portrayal of James Bond, Connery played the secret service agent in seven films.

SUNDAY 26th AUGUST 1923

A factory worker named Mary Hunter, aged 17 who resided at 10 Salamander Street, Leith, was suddenly seized by faintness while looking out of her window and fell some 30 feet to the ground below. The girl, who received serious leg injuries, was taken to Leith Hospital where she had to be detained.

WEDNESDAY 27th AUGUST 1567

James Stewart, Earl of Moray and a half-brother of Mary Queen of Scots, was proclaimed Regent of Scotland at a ceremony in Edinburgh, after Queen Mary had abdicated and fled to England.

WEDNESDAY 28th AUGUST 1929

Thomas Hill, aged 56 of 7 Wheatfield Road, Edinburgh, died in the Royal Infirmary this afternoon as a result of injuries received from a street fall. He was standing on a car island at the east end of Shandwick Place when he stumbled and fell backwards, striking his head on the road.

SUNDAY 29th AUGUST 1784

James Tytler, a chemist and writer, made Britain's first-ever manned flight in his Grand Edinburgh Fire Balloon, taking off in Holyrood Park and landing at Restalrig.

MONDAY 29th AUGUST 1910

In Edinburgh City Police Court, William Hedderwick, a 50-year-old gardener from Causewayside, Edinburgh, appeared in answer to a charge of having on Saturday night behaved in a disorderly manner and threatened to commit suicide, and also with having attempted later to commit suicide in his house by hanging. He pleaded guilty to the charge. Cullen sent the accused to prison for 30 days.

FRIDAY 30th AUGUST 1929

A nine-month old dog, against which viciousness was alleged, was given a chance to redeem itself when its owner, a woman, appeared in Edinburgh Police Court in its defence. The prosecutor said the dog had bitten a little boy of seven who had been playing on the street and had been anxious to be friendly with the animal. On a previous occasion it had savaged a woman. The owner, having indicated her fondness for the dog and her willingness to rehabilitate it, was given one month by the court in which to 'correct its behaviour', or it would be seized and destroyed.

TUESDAY 30th AUGUST 1949

A dangerous drugs warning was put out by Edinburgh City Police. Apparently, between 9.30am and 10am, a small tube containing ten morphine hydrochloride tablets was lost on a tramcar between Colinton Road, Tollcross and Craiglockhart Avenue. 'The tablets look like saccharin tablets and are dangerous if they fall into the hands of children,' stated the police.

SUNDAY 31st AUGUST 1941

Thousands of Edinburgh citizens were in Princes Street rehearsing for the possible gas attacks Nazi pre-war propaganda once suggested. Under the control of the local air defence authorities and the military, the exercise went well, and those who forgot to put their masks on in time ended up with streaming eyes as the tear gas – specially chosen for the exercise – disorientated them. The exercise was dubbed a success and coincided with similar events in Scotland's other cities.

SEPTEMBER

SATURDAY 1st SEPTEMBER AD714

St Giles, Edinburgh's patron saint and the man whom the city's cathedral was named after, died of an unknown illness. He was renowned for his miracles and sanctity.

THURSDAY 1st SEPTEMBER 1558

The St Giles's Day celebrations in Edinburgh went ahead as planned, despite the theft of the statue of the city's titular saint – widely believed to be the work of preacher John Knox in an attempt to undermine Catholicism.

WEDNESDAY 2nd SEPTEMBER 1925

At nearby North Berwick, a lady visitor named Miss Flint got into difficulties swimming, and but for the prompt and gallant act of William Logan, a golf professional, she would probably have lost her life. Finding herself being carried away by a fast running tide, she cried out for assistance, and Logan swam out and kept her up until both were picked up by a motor launch and landed safely back at the harbour.

FRIDAY 2nd SEPTEMBER 1949

Westerlea, a residential treatment centre and school for spastic children, in Ellersley Road, Edinburgh, was formerly opened by Her Royal Highness the Princess Royal. It was the first school of its kind in Scotland and the second in Britain. Addressing the large gathering which had assembled at the side entrance to the house, Her Royal Highness said the vision, enthusiasm, and quiet effort behind the planning of the scheme to have in Scotland a school for the care of spastics must command their deep admiration. Their sympathy went out to all disabled children.

TUESDAY 3rd SEPTEMBER 1650

The Scottish Church's purging – on religious grounds – of the Scottish Army's officers after meetings in Edinburgh backfired spectacularly. Well-equipped but poorly led, the Scottish Army blundered to a catastrophic defeat to Cromwell's invading English Army at Dunbar, despite beginning the battle with both a numerical and a territorial advantage. Most Scots soldiers who were taken prisoner were sent to the West Indies as slaves by Cromwell.

THE ICONIC FORTH BRIDGE

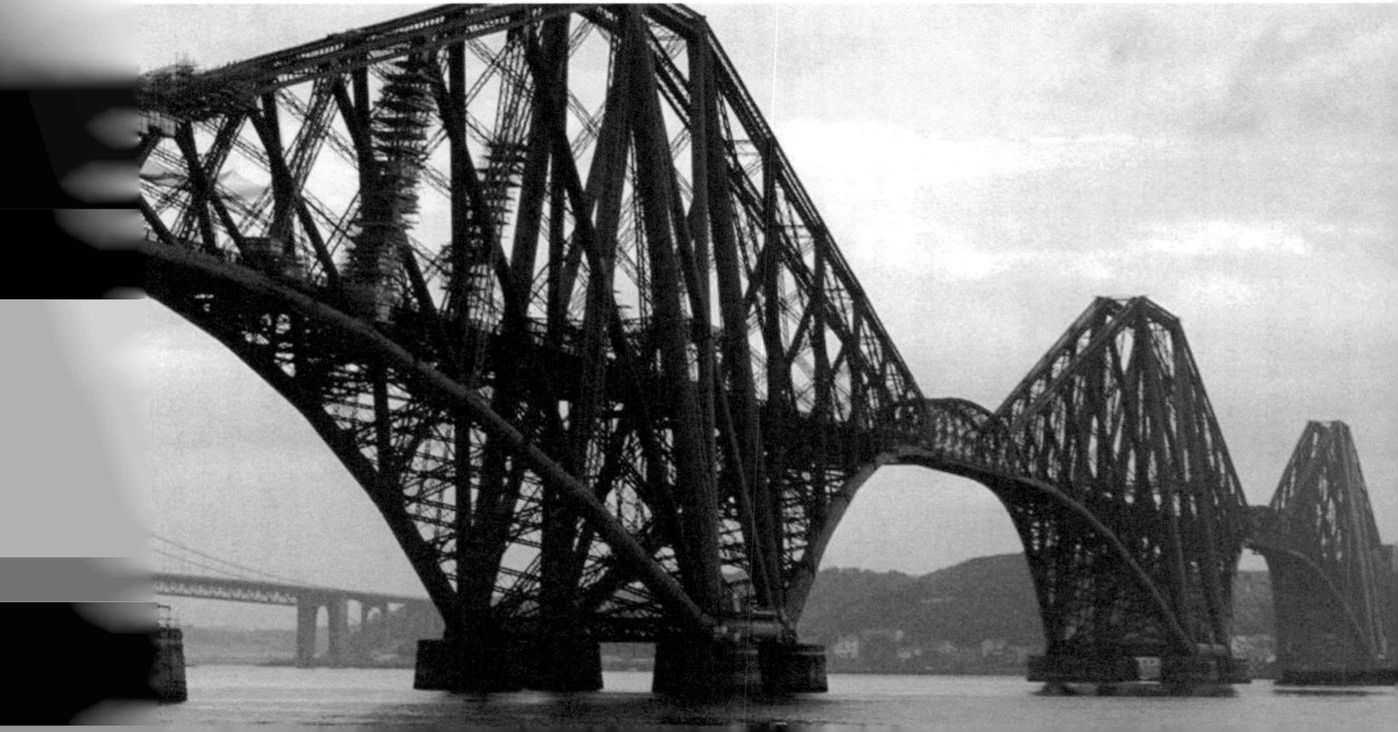

FRIDAY 4th SEPTEMBER 1964

Around 100,000 people turned out to see the Queen open the new £19.5m Forth Road Bridge. There was a naval gun salute and much cheering. The toll was set at 12-and-a-half pence. The structure is over 2.5 km long and 39,000 tonnes of steel and 125,000 cubic metres of concrete were used in its construction.

TUESDAY 5th SEPTEMBER 1648

Edinburgh Castle was seized by the Earl of Eglinton, a leader of the Whiggamores, a radical Presbyterian movement drawn, largely, from the south-west of Scotland.

TUESDAY 5th SEPTEMBER 1899

A draft of the 1st Battalion Gordon Highlanders, consisting of two officers, two NCOs and 98 men, left Edinburgh en route to India. The officers were Second Lieutenants Murray and Best, and the detachment was made up almost entirely of young men who had not previously seen any foreign service. There were no Dargai heroes among them, and only one man, Sergeant Paterson, has previously been in India. The draft paraded within the castle at about nine o'clock and, headed by the pipe band, they marched to Waverley Station by the Castle-hill, Lawnmarket, Bank Street, The Mound and the Waverley Bridge. The Esplanade was closed to the public and a crowd of over 1,000 congregated to give the young soldiers a cordial send-off, while hundreds of people lined the route to the station.

MONDAY 6th SEPTEMBER 1909

An Edinburgh labourer with 12 previous convictions appeared at Edinburgh Sheriff Court charged with a hideous assault on a woman in the Canongate. Alexander Simpson admitted punching the woman, dragging her around the house by her hair and assaulting her with a red-hot poker. He was sent to prison for three months.

MONDAY 7th SEPTEMBER 1903

Police requested that anyone with information regarding the recent sabotage on Balerno Rail Terminus on the outskirts of the city present themselves. Signal boxes had been set ablaze and telegraph wires had been cut – by persons unknown for reasons unknown – greatly jeopardising the safety of passengers on locomotives using the line.

MONDAY 7th SEPTEMBER 1964

Education in Edinburgh received a major boost with the opening of Napier Technical College.

WEDNESDAY 8th SEPTEMBER 1715

Amid the Jacobite rebellion, pro-Stuart rebels led by Lord Drummond attempted to capture Edinburgh Castle, using a scaling ladder at night, aided by three Jacobite sympathisers within the garrison. The plot failed when Drummond and his men spent most of the afternoon and evening in Edinburgh taverns, toasting their imminent success. They made too much noise when attempting their escalade and the alarm was soon sounded with 20 government troops sent to investigate. Drummond and his men escaped unmolested but the three soldiers who tried to assist them from within the fortress were tried for treason. One of them, a Private William Ainslie, was immediately hanged on the very spot from which he and his co-conspirators had lowered the ladder.

SATURDAY 8th SEPTEMBER 1736

John Porteous, Captain of the Town Guard, was snatched from his prison cell by an angry mob and hanged from a dye-pole. He had been awaiting trial after his men had fired on the crowd at a public hanging, killing or wounding 30 people. The mob had feared Porteous would be given a light sentence for ordering the shootings, so they took matters into their own hands.

FRIDAY 9th SEPTEMBER 1937

Wrapped in a piece of blanket and two pieces of a cotton sheet, a newly-born male child was found lying on the grass at the side of the road near Colinton. The child was stated to be strong and healthy. He was taken to Craiglockhart Poorhouse Hospital, where he was cared for. Meanwhile investigations were being made by the police in an attempt to trace the mother of the child.

SATURDAY 9th SEPTEMBER 1978

Hugh MacDiarmid, the famous Scottish author, poet and one of the founders of the Scottish National Party, died in Edinburgh, his adopted home. His real name was Christopher Grieve.

SATURDAY 10th SEPTEMBER 1547

A poorly armed but highly motivated Scots army marched out of Edinburgh to do battle with the English at Pinkie – they were swiftly annihilated. The battle was sparked by English demands that Edward VI of England (aged 10) should marry Mary Queen of Scots (aged 5) – an event known as the 'Rough Wooing'. It was estimated that 15,000 Scots were killed, 1,500 captured and English losses amounted to only 500 killed or wounded.

MONDAY 10th SEPTEMBER 2007

The trial of a convicted killer and sex offender who was accused of murdering two young women in Edinburgh 30 years ago collapsed. Angus Sinclair had denied attacking and killing 17-year-olds Christine Eadie and Helen Scott in what became known as the 'World's End' murders case. The girls were last seen in the World's End pub in the city and their bodies dumped in East Lothian in October 1977. Judge Lord Clarke said the Crown had insufficient evidence to proceed.

WEDNESDAY 11th SEPTEMBER 1745

The Jacobite army of Bonnie Prince Charlie captured Edinburgh without firing a single shot, after using a cunning ruse to get the Town Guard to open the city gates. The castle and its arsenal remained in government hands though. No-one was injured in the brief action, save for a Town Guardsman who was trampled and bruised.

FRIDAY 11th SEPTEMBER 1992

With the UK Government holding the EU Presidency, the European Summit between the 12 member states was held in Holyrood House in the capital. The delegates discussed vital issues such as the future of the EC, including immigration. Prime Minister John Major was the man who chose Edinburgh as the setting for this historic meeting, the culmination of the UK's presidency.

TUESDAY 12th SEPTEMBER 1848

William McNab, curator of the Royal Botanic Gardens, died. He was responsible for 'greening' Scotland in the 19th century. He moved 4,000 plant species, including trees from a site on Leith Walk, to the site of the present gardens at Inverleith.

THURSDAY 12th SEPTEMBER 1946

Work was begun on the erection of the new BBC transmitter near Granton Gasworks in Edinburgh. The transmitter would at first be used on an experimental basis but the ultimate aim was to use it for the 'third programme'.

THURSDAY 13th SEPTEMBER 1923

A full warrant to erect six three-storey tenements in the Wardie housing area was granted to the Edinburgh Corporation at a sitting of Edinburgh Dean of Guild Court. The houses, of which there would be 35 in all, would be of three apartments each. It was hoped their construction would alleviate overcrowding in Edinburgh.

SUNDAY 13th SEPTEMBER 1942

Severely wounded in the head by a buckshot rifle, Mrs Cecilia Sunshine of 29 High Street, Prestonpans was admitted to Edinburgh Royal Infirmary. Mrs Sunshine, who was 19 years of age, was conveyed to the infirmary by Red Cross ambulance. The circumstances under which she received the gunshot wound remain a mystery.

TUESDAY 14th SEPTEMBER 1507

Edinburgh's merchants were granted the exclusive privilege of running a printing press. They were called Chapman and Millar.

TUESDAY 14th SEPTEMBER 1993

A battling performance saw Hearts beat Atlético Madrid, 2-1, in a thrilling Uefa Cup first-leg tie at Tynecastle. Goals from John Colquhoun and John Robertson had the home side on easy street before a stunning strike by Polish international striker Roman Kosecki, against the run of play, changed the complexion of the tie, and left the Jambos with a difficult, but by no means impossible, task to face in the second leg.

FRIDAY 15th SEPTEMBER 1595

A City Baillie was shot when Edinburgh High School pupils rioted after they were refused a holiday. King James expressed his 'surprise' at the incident which, at the time, was unprecedented.

TUESDAY 15th SEPTEMBER 1640

After a four-month siege, the Royalist garrison in Edinburgh Castle was forced to surrender due to lack of provisions. They had withstood escalades, and even a huge mine being exploded under the walls by the besiegers, but the threat of starvation compelled them to finally throw in the towel. Two hundred innocent townspeople had been killed during the siege by stray cannonballs and shot.

THURSDAY 16th SEPTEMBER 2004

A crowd of 19,000 Hearts fans attended Murrayfield to see their side take on Portuguese outfit Braga in a Uefa Cup first-leg tie. Braga's coach had been talking up his side all week, so it was all the sweeter for the Jambos when they won the match 3-1 with goals from Andy Webster, Patrick Kisnorbo and Paul Hartley. The Gorgie side were now within touching distance of the new, lucrative group stages of the revamped competition.

THURSDAY 16th SEPTEMBER 2010

Pope Benedict XVI touched down in Edinburgh as part of his UK visit, where he met the Queen and Scotland's First Minister Alex Salmond at Holyrood. Around 125,000 people lined the route of his cavalcade as Il Papa waved to joyous pilgrims and even sported a scarf bearing a green tartan specially designed for his visit. He was then taken to Bellahouston Park in Glasgow where he held open-air Mass.

FRIDAY 17th SEPTEMBER 1745

Prince Charles Edward Stuart took up residence in Holyrood Palace, where he charmed visitors and held several impressive balls. On the same day, 200 men from Edinburgh under John Roy Stewart joined his army, far fewer than the Prince had expected from the capital.

WEDNESDAY 17th SEPTEMBER 1975

Hibs boss Eddie Turnbull vowed his team would score at Anfield after the Hibees narrowly beat English giants Liverpool 1-0 in a Uefa Cup first-round, first-leg tie at Easter Road. Liverpool goalkeeper Ray Clemence saved a John Brownlie penalty and Liverpool had a goal chalked off. Joe Harper scored the only goal of the game.

THURSDAY 18th SEPTEMBER 1924

Mr Alfred Lugg, general secretary of the Actors' Association, who had arrived in Edinburgh in connection with the campaign against the Stage Guild and the attempted boycott of Sir John Martin Harvey, addressed a meeting outside the Lyceum Theatre. The meeting attracted a considerable crowd, but nothing disorderly occurred. The dispute continued.

MONDAY 18th SEPTEMBER 1950

An attraction for Edinburgh holiday crowds was the five-ton Mercedes-Benz car which belonged to Hermann Goering during World War II. There were queues at the SMT Sales and Service showroom in Lothian Road for most of the day of people waiting to see the vehicle, which was complete with an effigy of the Field-Marshal. The car, which would be on view at the showroom until the following Saturday, was now owned by the Soldiers', Sailors' and Airmen's Families' Association, and had been brought to Edinburgh with the object of raising funds for the organisation. It took careful manoeuvring to get the car, which was 20-feet long, into position. The vehicle was powered by an eight-cylinder double-plugged engine, normally developing 155 horsepower but rising to 230 horsepower when the supercharger was in use. The bodywork was heavily armoured, and there was a mine shield below the body. The windows and windscreen were made of bulletproof Jena glass, by now splintered as a result of point-blank firing by disbelieving soldiers.

MONDAY 19th SEPTEMBER 1949

Edinburgh police were still making inquiries for the man who took £62 from a visiting Aberdeen team by a confidence trick. At Goldenacre Rugby ground one Saturday the man went round the visiting team – Aberdeen Grammar School – with a satchel stating that he would take their valuables for 'safe keeping' and the visitors, thinking he was on the home staff, handed over their wallets, the contents of which totalled £62. The con man was described as between 35 and 40 with greying hair receding at the temple. He was wearing a blue sports jacket and flannel trousers. Though not considered dangerous at all, police still advised the public not to attempt apprehending the man on their own.

TUESDAY 20th SEPTEMBER 1927

The Scottish Motor Traction Company's garage at Fountainbridge, Edinburgh, was the scene of an alarming outbreak of fire at about 5am. Several buses were damaged, two of them badly. One of the employees, Ian Dempster, a labourer from 47 Montrose Terrace, Edinburgh, was burned about the hands and legs, and later had his injuries attended to at the Royal Infirmary. It was understood the fire occurred while Dempster was engaged at a petrol tank. His lamp broke, igniting the petrol gases, and causing an explosion. When two fire engines arrived, two buses were in flames. Working in co-operation, the employees and firemen found their work handicapped owing to the heavy pall of smoke and the dense fumes. The firemen were unable to use their flares. After working for an hour, the employees and firemen finally subdued the flames, and the buses were driven out into the street. An extractor was put into operation, and the building was speedily cleared of fumes. The damage to the building was not serious.

SATURDAY 21st SEPTEMBER 1745

Prince Charles Edward Stuart's Jacobite army destroyed the government army of Sir John Cope at the battle of Prestonpans, just outside Edinburgh, after a local man named Anderson had guided the Jacobites through a bog so they could attack the government troops from a more favourable position. Around 300 redcoats were killed and the remainder of the 2,500-strong government army was either wounded or taken prisoner, with Cope and a few hundred of his dragoons being the only escapees. The Jacobites lost 50 men in the 15-minute engagement.

SUNDAY 21st SEPTEMBER 2008

Hundreds of people living in the Sighthill area of Edinburgh watched the demolition of a block of notorious 1960s high-rise flats. The tall block, considered an eyesore by many, came down shortly before midday as a 600-strong crowd looked on. Broomview Court was demolished as part of a housing regeneration drive for the city. It had stood since 1967 but, like other high rise schemes, it had been synonymous with deprivation, drug abuse and deep social problems. Next on the council's demolition agenda were the high-rise blocks at Gracemount.

FRIDAY 22nd SEPTEMBER 1933

The Palais de Danse, Fountainbridge, was reopened for the new season. The great ballroom presented a stimulating spectacle. Close to a thousand dancers attended, and the floor, accordingly, during the dances, might easily be said to have been filled to capacity. At an early stage of the programme, a 'Paul Jones' dance was engaged, and served to get revellers moving. There appeared to be no new dances this year, popular interest being satisfied with the foxtrot, waltz, rhumba, and the tango. The Magistracy and the Town Council of the city were represented, and those attending also included a number of city officials.

WEDNESDAY 23rd SEPTEMBER 1925

Mr Stuart Pilcher, manager of Edinburgh Corporation Tramways, submitted a proposal at a meeting of a Tramways Sub-Committee of Edinburgh Town Council to run a night service of motor buses in the city. It was agreed to recommend to the Tramways Committee that the scheme be tried as an experiment. The proposal was to run buses every 49 minutes after the ordinary car service stopped, and that the route to be tried should be from the foot of Leith Walk to Tollcross, and from Haymarket to Salisbury Place. The minimum fare would be 6d. It was thought a night bus service would be a considerable convenience to dancers, who at the time had either to walk home or hire a taxi. At the same meeting, it was also agreed that all Edinburgh tram workers should learn the new international language of Esperanto. The language was created in the late 1870s and early 1880s by Dr Ludwig Lazarus Zamenhof, from Bialystok, then part of the Russian Empire.

MONDAY 24th SEPTEMBER 1923

The inauguration of the new clock at the slaughterhouse at Gorgie took place, when Treasurer Stevenson, one of the representatives of the Gorgie Ward on Edinburgh Town Council, set the clock going in the presence of a gathering which included members of the Market Committee of the Town Council, workers in the slaughter-house, and members of the general public. The clock, which occupied a prominent position, stood on a beautifully ornamented pillar, and was surmounted by a representation of the city coat of arms.

FRIDAY 24th SEPTEMBER 1965

Captain Leonard Gellatly, a farm worker on the Margell Estate, warned the public to keep their pets under control after five sheep were killed by dogs on the site. Mr Gellatly was said to be making regular patrols of the fields and had threatened to shoot dogs on sight. This was the second time in as many years that Mr Gellatly has been forced to issue such a warning.

MONDAY 25th SEPTEMBER 1939

Seven persons appeared before Sheriff Jamieson at Edinburgh Sheriff Court for offences against the lighting regulations during the blackout hours. A shopkeeper with premises in the centre of the town was fined 30s. Another offender was fined 25s. Four fines of 10s and one of 5s were also imposed. The majority of the offences were minor contraventions of the regulations. One defendant likened ARP wardens to Gestapo officers.

TUESDAY 25th SEPTEMBER 1945

Edinburgh prepared to celebrate the end of the war in style with some Royal guests of honour. Flags were put up on public buildings and shopkeepers and many householders were busy decorating their premises and homes with 'gay bunting'. Everything was ready for the two-day Royal visit to the Scottish capital. The king and queen arrived at Princes Street Station that morning at ten o'clock and, following two investitures at the Palace of Holyroodhouse, the king took the salute at the Mound at three o'clock in connection with the big Victory Parade along Princes Street. Thousands of people lined the streets of the capital.

FRIDAY 26th SEPTEMBER 1924

The commencement of the construction of the new Edinburgh and Glasgow road at the Edinburgh end was the occasion of an interesting open-air ceremony. Members of the Corporation, and representatives of other local authorities and of the Ministry of Transport, gathered in the sunshine of a perfect autumn day at the junction of the Bathgate and Linlithgow roads, about one mile west of Corstorphine, where the ceremonies of cutting the first sod, and of placing a memorial stone in position, were undertaken.

EDINBURGH CASTLE'S ESPLANADE

TUESDAY 26th SEPTEMBER 1989

Hibs' first European foray in 11 years ended in triumph as the Easter Road men defeated Hungarian side Videoton 3-0 in Hungary to win their Uefa Cup tie 4-0 on aggregate. Goals from Keith Houchen, Gareth Evans and John Collins completed the impressive display in front of 17,000 fans.

FRIDAY 27th SEPTEMBER 1940

Luftwaffe bombs fell onto the lawn of the Palace of Holyroodhouse, creating a huge crater. Though no-one was injured, a gardener complained that the Nazis had 'dug it up' just after he had redesigned it.

TUESDAY 28th SEPTEMBER 1937

A bull which broke away from Bonnyrigg slaughterhouse created considerable excitement before it was recaptured. It careered along the public highway, entered a field and subsequently ran on to the main railway line to the south. The driver of an express from Edinburgh Waverley to London had to draw up at Lothian Bridge to avoid running it down. The animal was frightened off the track and went on to the embankment, where it tossed a butcher who tried to get it under control. The animal proceeded to a vacant piece of ground at Newtongrange, and defied capture. A local farmer drove six of his own bullocks on to the ground, and managed to herd them all back to the farm.

THURSDAY 28th SEPTEMBER 2000

A crowd of 15,000 Heart of Midlothian fans packed Tynecastle to witness a famous European night in the Uefa Cup. The injury-ravaged Jambos almost pulled off a stunning victory over German crack side VfB Stuttgart, and the tie couldn't have been closer. Trailing 1-0 from the first leg in Germany, Hearts took the lead through Steven Pressley after 16 minutes but the German side equalised 20 minutes later, before taking the lead after 57 minutes. Colin Cameron scored a penalty for Hearts late on to add to a Gordan Petric goal, meaning Hearts just needed one more goal to progress to the next round. Alas, Petric was saint turned sinner as he missed a sitter in the last minute, sending Stuttgart – who had been reduced to nine men – through on the away goals rule.

SUNDAY 29th SEPTEMBER 1940

A heavy Luftwaffe raid saw a two-storey housing block in West Pilton flattened, killing an 8-year-old boy named Ronald MacArthur, and mortally wounding his younger sister.

TUESDAY 29th SEPTEMBER 1992

Hibs slumped out of the Uefa Cup on away goals after drawing 1-1 with Belgian side Anderlecht in Brussels. Darren Jackson's goal cancelled out Luc Nilis's earlier strike but it wasn't enough for Alex Miller's men, who had drawn the first leg at Easter Road 2-2.

THURSDAY 30th SEPTEMBER 1926

Luigi Di Placedo, a middle-aged Italian of 120 Buccleuch Street, Edinburgh, was charged at Edinburgh Sheriff Court with having a six-chambered revolver and six live cartridges in his house without holding a firearms certificate. On being fined 2s he stated, through an interpreter, that he had no money to pay the fine, and was allowed a fortnight in which to find the money. Mr William Horn the Fiscal stated it was highly desirable that the revolver and cartridges should be removed from the house, as they had been found lying on a shelf where they could be got at by anyone. He asked that the firearm and ammunition should be confiscated. Placedo, who did not speak English, intimated he had nothing to say, and Sheriff Jamieson ordered the revolver and cartridges to be confiscated.

THURSDAY 30th SEPTEMBER 1943

When the fire brigade was summoned to an outbreak of fire in a top-flat house at 60 Candlemaker Row, Edinburgh, the firemen found the occupant Mary Clark, aged 75 and a retired school teacher, lying behind the kitchen door. She had received severe burning injuries to the head and face, and was certified dead on being removed to the Royal Infirmary. The deceased lived alone in the house.

OCTOBER

FRIDAY 1st OCTOBER 1568

The Bannatyne Manuscript, the most extensive collection of early Scottish poetry in existence, was published by George Bannatyne, a well-to-do Edinburgh merchant.

WEDNESDAY 1st OCTOBER 1788

William 'Deacon' Brodie was hanged with his associate George Smith at Edinburgh's Tolbooth. A respectable businessman, carpenter and high ranking city councillor, Brodie, in fact, lived a double life as a serial burglar in order to fund his decadent gambling habits. As a member of Edinburgh's 'in crowd' he easily knew which houses in Edinburgh contained the richest pickings. After he and Smith were betrayed by another gang member, called Ainslie, the game was up. Brodie tried to cheat death on the gallows by having a primitive type of tracheotomy done to prevent asphyxiation, with tacit approval of the bribed hangman, but he died from the hanging anyway, though many rumours of his supposed miraculous revival and clandestine escape persisted for years after his death.

WEDNESDAY 2nd OCTOBER 1940

There were a large number of mourners at the crematorium on Warriston Road, Edinburgh, for the two little victims of a recent Luftwaffe air raid. The tragic children of Mr and Mrs A McArthur were Ronald aged seven, and his five-year-old sister Morag.

SUNDAY 3rd OCTOBER 1706

The Scottish Parliament met for the last time in Edinburgh before its historic union with the English Parliament at Westminster.

TUESDAY 3rd OCTOBER 1944

A shortage of milk supplies was being experienced in Edinburgh today. It was attributed to the cold weather, which had affected production. The scarcity was expected to continue for some days. An official of a large dairy company in the city stated that producers were having difficulty in maintaining supplies, which in some cases had been curtailed by amounts varying from 10 to 25%, daily. This meant a reduction in supplies to non-priority consumers.

WEDNESDAY 4th OCTOBER 1916

Caulkers employed by a Leith shipbuilding firm were charged with bad timekeeping before the Edinburgh and District Munitions Tribunal. One worker, who had lost 54 hours out of a possible 108, claimed he had lost two days because his tools had gone missing, while the rest of his 'lost time' was due to the fact his mother was away on holiday and he therefore had no-one to wake him in the mornings.

THURSDAY 4th OCTOBER 2001

The brand-new Ocean Terminal shopping centre in Leith first opened its doors. It was built on former industrial docklands on the north side of the city at the edge of the boundary between the formerly separate ports of Leith and Newhaven. The land was formerly occupied by the Henry Robb shipyard, which closed in 1983.

WEDNESDAY 5th OCTOBER 1785

The Italian Vincenzo Lunardi wowed 80,000 spectators in Edinburgh by performing Scotland's first-ever hydrogen hot air balloon lift-off, landing in Fife some 35 minutes later.

THURSDAY 5th OCTOBER 1950

The new session of the Edinburgh Parliament, which follows the procedure of the House of Commons, opened in the Dean of Guild Courtroom, City Chambers, with the formation of the Government and questions to ministers. This public debating society, which met every Thursday evening from October to March, had a 'Strangers' Gallery' which was open to the public. On enrolment members were allotted a 'constituency', and took their place in the party of their choice.

FRIDAY 6th OCTOBER 1950

An orang-utan at the Edinburgh Zoo attacked and injured the assistant manager, Mr Brooke Cunliffe of 22 Belgrave Road, Edinburgh. The animal caught Mr Cunliffe's hand in its jaws and lacerated it severely. The ape then beat its chest in a show of defiance before it was subdued by staff. Cunliffe was removed to the Royal Infirmary, where he was later stated to be in a satisfactory condition, though a little shaken by the ordeal.

FRIDAY 6th OCTOBER 1995

Powderhall Stadium closed for the last time, despite a 10,000 signature petition against its closure being submitted to the council. Owner Eddie Ramsay had in turn pointed out that if the 10,000 signatories had bothered attending the greyhound racing, speedway and other events there, there would be no need for it to be sold in the first place. The site has been earmarked for housing development.

FRIDAY 7th OCTOBER 1932

The North British Aviation Company announced plans to hold an air pageant at Duddingston Mains that weekend. The display would include wing-walking, crazy-flying and parachute descents. Captain Fresson would co-ordinate events and be in charge of the flying.

MONDAY 7th OCTOBER 1940

Housing in Marchmont was severely damaged by four high-explosive bombs during a Luftwaffe air-raid on Edinburgh.

SUNDAY 8th OCTOBER 1916

A hospital train arrived at Edinburgh Caledonian Station carrying 171 wounded soldiers, who were in turn conveyed to four hospitals; Deaconess, Craigleith, Leith War Hospital and Dalmenny House. Newington House in Edinburgh was then instructed to reorganise its premises to deal with those soldiers who had been blinded.

WEDNESDAY 8th OCTOBER 1930

A joint committee of Edinburgh Town Council visited Saughton Gardens to investigate a site being found there for the Gladstone statue, the removal of which from St Andrew Square was proposed. The committee approved of a site in one of the rose gardens, and a recommendation to that effect would now come before the Town Council that week. Tenders for the removal of the statue were invited some time ago.

WEDNESDAY 9th OCTOBER 1963

Hearts took on Swiss outfit Lausanne at Tynecastle in the Inter-Cities Fairs Cup second leg. The Swiss side triumphed 3-2 after extra-time thanks to a Schneiter goal after 102 minutes, which meant Hearts were eliminated as the first leg had finished 2-2.

THURSDAY 9th OCTOBER 2003

The controversial new Edinburgh Royal Infirmary (ERI), which was initially dogged by problems since it opened its doors in January 2002, was officially opened by the Princess Royal. The £184 million hospital at Little France was supposed to be the finest in Europe but was dogged by technical problems and landed the health authority in millions of pounds in debt. The ERI was built by the Consort Healthcare Consortium, which was made up of Balfour Beatty Construction, Morrison Development and the Royal Bank of Scotland. Building began on the ERI site, three miles south of the city centre, in October 1998 and the first patients were admitted for surgery in January 2002. All patient services were transferred from the old Royal Infirmary at Lauriston Place between April and May of 2003.

SUNDAY 10th OCTOBER 1802

The Edinburgh Review was first published 'to erect a higher standard of merit, and secure a bolder and purer taste in literature, and to apply philosophical principles and the maxims of truth and humanity to politics'.

TUESDAY 10th OCTOBER 1922

A man named John Thomas Blair appeared at Edinburgh Sheriff Court on a charge of stealing a box containing 48 pairs of corsets from a hotel in George Street, Edinburgh. He pleaded guilty, and an agent stated the box was lifted from a landing in the hotel when Blair was the worse for drink. Previous convictions for house-breaking, larceny and theft were libelled against the accused, who was sentenced by Sheriff Nish to undergo imprisonment for three months.

TUESDAY 11th OCTOBER 1910

In an irate letter published in *The Scotsman*, an anonymous local resident complained bitterly about drunkenness and vagrancy in and around the High Street area. The resident, and her English friend, were subjected to torrents of foul-mouthed, drunken and lecherous abuse between St Giles and John Knox's House the previous day and finished their letter of complaint by asking, rhetorically, if such drunkenness would be tolerated in any other European capital city.

WEDNESDAY 11th OCTOBER 2000

Scotland's first First Minister, Donald Dewar MSP, died suddenly of a brain haemorrhage after a fall on the steps of his official residence in Edinburgh. He'd held that particular position for just 17 months.

MONDAY 12th OCTOBER 1942

The Prime Minister, Winston Churchill, made a flying visit to Edinburgh, and had the freedom of the city conferred upon him in the Usher Hall. With the country at war, no intimation in advance could be given of the Prime Minister's visit, and to the vast majority of the public it came as a surprise. Nevertheless, the news spread quickly, one of the first intimations being flags flying from some of the buildings in Princes Street.

THURSDAY 12th OCTOBER 1950

Just over 200 striking employees at the Edinburgh factory of Ferranti returned to work. Officials of their unions, the Electrical Trades and the Amalgamated Engineering, were to have discussions with the management in an effort to settle the trouble. The strikers had stopped work because a shop steward had been given seven days' notice on 'redundancy grounds' without consultation.

WEDNESDAY 13th OCTOBER 1909

While passing along Yeaman Bridge over the Union Canal, a workman observed what appeared to be the body of a man floating in the water some 30 yards away. He immediately informed the police, who after dragging the object from the water discovered the workman's assumption was indeed correct. The deceased was identified as William Wood, 50 years of age, a cabman, who resided at nearby 156 Dundee Street.

FRIDAY 13th OCTOBER 1972

Ernst Dumoulin, a Dutchman, married his German fiancé Helga Konrad in Haymarket Registrar's Office. The immigrant couple's joy was short-lived, however, as Ernst threw his new wife off Salisbury Crags later that afternoon, in an attempt to cash in on a near half-million pound life-insurance policy that he had taken out on her. The Dutchman claimed his wife had fallen accidentally.

THURSDAY 14th OCTOBER 1926

Edinburgh Dean of Guild Court granted a warrant to the British Linen Bank for the erection of a new building at 140-141 Princes Street. The new premises, which were expected to be ready for use in about 18 months, would replace one of the oldest bank buildings in Scotland. When the application was put before the court, Councillor Baxter, a member of the court, remarked that; "The more it was delayed the better, as fair Princes Street was being ruined with banks."

THURSDAY 14th OCTOBER 1943

Mrs Anne Fraser launched 'Women for Westminster', a group whose main objective was to train women to stand as candidates at the next general election. Back then there were only 14 female MPs, compared to 601 male MPs.

TUESDAY 15th OCTOBER 1912

About 800 carters in Edinburgh and Leith came out on strike, as the arbitration arrangements fell through and no settlement of the dispute was arrived at. About 500 of the strikers were employed by the general and railway contractors in Leith, the remainder being employees of Edinburgh railway contractors.

THURSDAY 15th OCTOBER 1925

At a meeting of the Edinburgh and Leith Master Bakers' Association, it was resolved to reduce the price of bread by ½d, to 9½d on a four-pound loaf the following Monday. The decision followed a fall in the price of flour the previous day, when the cost per sack was lowered from 46s to 45s. A 'd' was a penny and there were ten to a shilling, and 20 shillings to a pound.

THURSDAY 16th OCTOBER 1924

The petition of the Scottish Rugby Union for a warrant to proceed with the erection of a grandstand on the new Roseburn Ground was continued at a meeting of Edinburgh Dean of Guild Court. Mr David Grieve, interim Dean of Guild, said the court required certain details as to girders, piers, and supports for the roof before granting warrant. It was hoped the new facilities would attract more supporters.

MONDAY 16th OCTOBER 1939

No explanation was offered as to why the city's warning sirens did not sound when 14 German Heinkels and Dorniers flew in at low altitude to attack warships in the Firth of Forth. Sixteen Navy men died and 44 were wounded. The Luftwaffe dropped 12 bombs on the ships. Four enemy planes were shot down; three by the RAF, one by land-based anti-aircraft guns on the nearby Pentland Hills, where the battery was manned by volunteer gunners.

MONDAY 17th OCTOBER 1932

A one-legged painter appeared in court in Dunfermline – across the river – after an incident on the Forth Rail Bridge. Mr W Vast of Orchard Brae, Edinburgh, pleaded guilty to causing an obstruction by refusing to leave the bridge when asked to do so by a watchman. Mr Vast explained he had lost his lower leg during the war and had missed the last train home on the evening in question, so had been in a state of distress when confronted by the watchman, who was ultimately forced to telephone Dalmeny Forth police who came and arrested the artist. Vast was fined 10 shillings, and ordered to pay expenses of 15 shillings and 6d.

THURSDAY 17th OCTOBER 1935

An addition to the Eventide Homes for old people, conducted by the Salvation Army, was formally opened in Edinburgh by Mrs Bramwell Booth. Through an anonymous gift of £7,000 the Army were able to purchase, furnish, and equip the commodious house at 29 South Oswald Road, which, named Sunnyside, would now accommodate 50 old people.

WEDNESDAY 18th OCTOBER 1939

"I am not satisfied with the explanation," said Lord Provost Steele in Edinburgh, commenting on the statement made by the Prime Minister in the House of Commons on the absence of an air-raid warning in Edinburgh during the attack by German bombers on the Firth of Forth that Monday. Hundreds of Edinburgh townsfolk had lucky escapes in the surprise raid, ranging from bullets striking their armchairs to shrapnel splinters blowing off chimneys.

A GUNNER'S EYE VIEW OF EDINBURGH AND THE FORTH ESTUARY, FROM EDINBURGH CASTLE'S RAMPARTS

MONDAY 19th OCTOBER 1931

A man charged in the Edinburgh Court with having been drunk and incapable pleaded for a chance, and asked to be allowed to go to 'the grubber' instead of being sent to prison. This slightly mystified the court, and it was explained that 'the grubber' was another name for the poorhouse. The man admitted that he was a methylated spirit drinker, and said that if he were allowed to stay in the poorhouse until after the New Year it might cure him of his bad habit. A dismissive Barbour Simpson imposed a fine of £2, or 20 days' imprisonment.

FRIDAY 19th OCTOBER 1945

Bert Couzens, the long-distance walker, arrived in Fleet Street, London, at 6.50am, beating his own 1937 record for the Edinburgh to London walk by nine hours 10 minutes. His time for the 408-mile course was 84 hours 50 minutes. During the whole walk he had only one hour 40 minutes' rest, and that was with no sleep. Looking fairly fresh, Couzens told a reporter who met him at the end of his trip; "Sleep? I won't be able to sleep for a couple of days. I believe I could beat even this new record if I tried." Couzens, who was accompanied by three cyclists, left Market Street in Edinburgh that Monday at 6pm and did the first lap non-stop to York, where he rested for an hour.

TUESDAY 20th OCTOBER 1925

What was described by the fiscal as 'a most unusual case of joyriding', came before Sheriff Jamieson at Edinburgh Sheriff Court, when three youths pleaded guilty to a charge that, on Thursday, 15th October, they broke into a garage in Portobello and sneakily took possession of a motor car, drove it to Port Edgar and South Queensferry and then abandoned it, leaving the car standing in a public highway. It was further stated they committed this offence knowing that the owner would not have allowed them to take possession of, and use, the car. The youths abandoned the car after crashing it into a wall, but two of them were admonished on account of the fact they came from 'respectable' families. The third accused and eldest of the three was fined 30s.

SUNDAY 21st OCTOBER 1571

John, Earl of Mar and Regent of Scotland, was forced to abandon his first siege of Edinburgh Castle, whose garrison and commander were still loyal to Queen Mary. Mar retired to Leith after little more than one week, having lost 100 of his best men. The castle's garrison had been commanded by Sir William Kirkcaldy of Grange. Grange was hanged two years later at the conclusion of a long siege.

THURSDAY 21st OCTOBER 1920

Leith Town Council met for the last time, and with one stroke of an administrator's pen Leith was swallowed up by the ever-expanding city of Edinburgh, after some 87 years as a separate Burgh. Gilmerton, Clermiston, Cramond and Trinity were also incorporated into the city boundary as part of the same 'deal'.

SUNDAY 22nd OCTOBER 2000

The live televised Edinburgh derby at Easter Road saw Andy Kirk and Colin Cameron score for Hearts – either side of six goals from rampant Hibs, including a hat-trick from Finnish striker Mixu Paatelainen and a gem of a goal by Russell Latapy. One of the loudest cheers of the night came when Cameron scored for Hearts late on to make it 6-2, though most of those who sarcastically cheered were in the Hibs end. John O'Neil and Frenchman David Zitelli were the Hibees' other scorers in the rout.

WEDNESDAY 23rd OCTOBER 1929

"Why don't you form yourselves into teams and play in the parks?" said Baillie Herbert Lindsay, when 22 boys appeared at Edinburgh Police Court. He stated that in all the cases the police had been acting on complaints from residents. Several of the offences were committed on Sundays. The Magistrate remarked that the people of Edinburgh were not going to be disturbed by boys playing football on the streets, and told the boys they must organise their games in a different way. There were public parks all over the city, and there was no necessity for them to disturb the citizens. He imposed a fine of 1s on boys who had previously been before the court, and admonished the others.

THURSDAY 24th OCTOBER 1861

The Edinburgh Co-operative Building Company began work on constructing dwellings at Reid Terrace. James Begg hailed the new works as "a turning point in the history of Edinburgh".

SUNDAY 24th OCTOBER 1993

Hibs took on Rangers in the League Cup Final at Celtic Park, aiming to win the trophy for the second time in two years. Despite a valiant effort, the Easter Road men lost the thrilling match 2-1 after a late wonder-goal by Ally McCoist. Ian Durrant had given the Ibrox side the lead just after half-time, but an own-goal by former Hearts player Dave McPherson had deservedly levelled the match before McCoist's audacious overhead kick took the cup back to Ibrox.

MONDAY 25th OCTOBER 1926

Throughout the day and during the night the storm in the middle and upper reaches of the Firth of Forth was the worst experienced for many years. A succession of fierce squalls, accompanied by blinding showers of rain, hail, and sleet, lashed the water into a flying spray. In the afternoon, along with the rising tide, the gale increased in fury, and heavy seas dashed themselves on beach and bulwark. A number of large steamers were anchored off Inchkeith, which normally provided a safe shelter during an easterly gale, but on this occasion such a wild sea was running that smaller craft were compelled to seek safety elsewhere. At Granton, the east breakwater was almost completely lost to view beneath the great waves which swept over it, while along the sea wall between Granton and Newhaven the water was thrown over the railway and into the street.

FRIDAY 26th OCTOBER 1917

Edinburgh experienced wintry weather. In the early hours snow began to fall and particularly in the forenoon there was heavy snow, with light showers of snow and rain in the afternoon. A cold wind blew from the north-west, and the temperature was 38.4 degrees. Such a low temperature had not occurred in an October month since the 31st October 1909. Drizzling rain fell in the evening, but despite the rain, all the roads out of the city remained blocked by snow.

WEDNESDAY 26th OCTOBER 1949

Detailed plans for the development of the St James's Square/
Leith Street area of Edinburgh were submitted by the City Town
Planning Officer, Mr D Plumstead, to a meeting of the Planning
Committee of the Town Council. In his report on the plans, Mr
Plumstead explained that the scheme was divided into four five-
year phases, and involved the re-housing of 1,200 families. The
area was zoned for commercial, office, entertainment and light
industry use. The district had some of the worst properties in the
city, consisting of a high percentage of slums, outmoded industrial
and commercial buildings, and a bad lay-out of roads. He stated
that, with few exceptions, the existing properties were pre-1895.

WEDNESDAY 27th OCTOBER 1943

Edinburgh Magistrates agreed on the recommendation of the
Edinburgh and Leith Wine, Spirit and Beer Trade Associations
that all public houses and bars licensed for the consumption of
liquor should be closed on Saturday, New Year's Day. The closing of
public houses on New Year's Day was introduced for the first time
on January 1st, 1943. Anti-drink and temperance campaigners in
Edinburgh expressed their approval of the move.

SUNDAY 27th OCTOBER 1985

John Blackley's Hibs team took on Aberdeen in the League Cup
Final at Hampden in front of over 40,000 fans. Sadly for those in
green and white who made the trip west, Hibs froze on the day
and lost the final 3-0, Billy Stark and Eric Black (2) scoring for
the Dons.

THURSDAY 28th OCTOBER 1937

One of the fascist candidates in the Edinburgh municipal elections
appeared at Edinburgh Sheriff Court, on a charge arising out of a
disturbance alleged to have occurred following a fascist meeting a
fortnight before. Five other young men also appeared in connection
with the affair. Pleas of not guilty were tendered in each case, and
a trial was fixed for December 9th. A youth of 16, who admitted a
charge of breach of the peace in connection with the disturbance,
was admonished. The fascist candidate was Richard Plathen.

THURSDAY 29th OCTOBER 1965

American singing sensation Gene Pitney played to a full house at the ABC Cinema, emulating his two sell-out gigs there the previous year. Fans had bombarded the venue with anxious enquiries in the seven days prior to the gig, after Pitney had been forced to cancel an appearance on TV's *Juke Box Jury* because of illness.

FRIDAY 29th OCTOBER 1915

Army recruitment officers in Edinburgh reported doing 'very good business' in the capital. Lord Derby's appeal to 'the manhood of the nation' had seen recruitment levels nearly double since 1914, with many coming from privileged families and being of 'serviceable type' and suitable to defend the country.

TUESDAY 30th OCTOBER 1923

Despite 22,000 signatures on a mercy petition, 'Mad' Phil Murray, a Princes Street newspaper vendor convicted of murdering a Dunfermline man, became the last man to be hanged in the city's Calton Jail.

MONDAY 31st OCTOBER 1932

The badly mutilated body of a man, found in the tunnel outside St Leonard's coal depot in Edinburgh, was later identified as Alexander Greig, a 52-year-old miner who resided at 7 King Street, Musselburgh.

TUESDAY 31st OCTOBER 1950

A Halloween bazaar held in the Music Hall, Edinburgh, raised over £300 for the funds of the Scottish Wayfarers' Welfare Society. Spookily, after about an hour of festivities, the lights in the hall went off momentarily, giving attendees a giggle, if not a fright.

NOVEMBER

WEDNESDAY 1st NOVEMBER 1769

A convicted murderer named Murdo Campbell – who was also a tax collector – cheated the noose by committing suicide in his cell before he could be executed. The Edinburgh mob, enraged at being denied the rare site of an exciseman twitching on the gallows, decided to seize his body anyway, and dragged it around Edinburgh for several hours before throwing it off the top of Salisbury Crags.

WEDNESDAY 1st NOVEMBER 1939

New anti-gas helmets – 7,600 in total – for babies were distributed in Edinburgh. At nearly 40 centres the work of fitting and demonstrating the helmet was undertaken. A police official stated to *The Scotsman* that children who were too big for the helmets would shortly be supplied with the special small-size respirator.

MONDAY 2nd NOVEMBER 1925

Fifteen motorists came before Sherriff Orr at Edinburgh Sherriff Court charged with speeding offences on Queensferry Road, Milton Road, Portobello Road and Osborne Terrace. The offenders had been caught doing between 21 and 50mph, and a fine of £2 each was imposed.

FRIDAY 2nd NOVEMBER 1951

An unemployed trawlerman appeared at Edinburgh Sheriff Court charged with stealing from Old St Paul's in Jeffrey Street. Andrew William Greg, a habitual thief with 13 previous convictions, was found to have stolen a sanctus bell, and two pairs of Sheffield plate candlesticks, but was caught when the rector saw the items in a broker's shop in the Canongate and informed the police. Mr Greg, 29, had sold the stolen goods for two shillings and sixpence and pleaded guilty as charged. Sheriff James Gilchrist sentenced the thief to 18 months' imprisonment.

WEDNESDAY 3rd NOVEMBER 1993

Plans for a 20,000-seater stadium to be leased by Hibs on a 100-acre site at Straiton adjacent to the Edinburgh City by-pass had been submitted for planning permission to Midlothian District Council. The first phase of the development was expected to cost around £8 million and involve 12,000 seats, with two other phases to follow.

MONDAY 3rd NOVEMBER 2003

Edinburgh played host to a gala-day of music that saw thousands of fans flock to the city for the MTV Europe Awards held in Leith, where Justin Timberlake, Christina Aguilera, Missy Elliot and Beyoncé all performed. Also on the bill was Jamaican RnB star Sean Paul, who also played a separate concert at the Corn Exchange afterwards.

WEDNESDAY 4th NOVEMBER 1925

A church parade was held by the Edinburgh Italian Fascist Section in commemoration of Italian Armistice Day. Fifty members dressed in black and marched to St Mary's Cathedral in Broughton Street where they heard Mass, and left their Italian flag and Union Jack at the altar. They were joined by members of the King's Own Scottish Borderers, whose piper played 'The Flowers of the Forest'.

MONDAY 4th NOVEMBER 1940

Two Luftwaffe bombs landed in the open at Edinburgh Zoo, though no staff or animals were injured in the botched raid. However, a large heap of dung was scattered by the explosion. In the same attack, a number of bombs also landed in Holyrood Park, much to the annoyance of gardeners. No-one was hurt.

WEDNESDAY 5th NOVEMBER 1997

A two-year-old boy was in hospital as a result of injuries received by fireworks in an accident at a display in Corstorphine. Graham Torrie, head of Lothian and Borders Fire Brigade, issued a statement informing the public that his officers were there to help, not to spoil their fun. This statement came in the wake of a marked increase in attacks on fire-crews by youths in Scotland.

TUESDAY 6th NOVEMBER 1934

John Gillies, a 32-year-old railway fireman who lived at 4 Dalgety Road, Edinburgh, met a horrible death at Duddingston Station, when he was attending to a lamp between the engines and wagons of a stationary train. He was crushed between the first wagon and the engine when another engine was being attached to the rear of the wagons.

MONDAY 6th NOVEMBER 1950

The need for civil defence was emphasised by Lord Provost Sir Andrew Murray at a press conference in Edinburgh City Chambers. He said the few hundred already enrolled in the city were not nearly enough for the required purposes. Recruits were required for headquarters, wardens, rescue, ambulance, pioneer and welfare sections, as well as for specialist roles like gunners, should the unthinkable 'third world war' happen.

SUNDAY 7th NOVEMBER 1920

Lord Salvesen unveiled a memorial in the Old Kirk, Canongate, Edinburgh, to the men of the congregation who fell in the Great War. The memorial, which was placed in the vestibule of the church, consists of a bronze tablet mounted on dark grey Carrara marble, inscribed with the names of 74 members who made the supreme sacrifice. The congregation's Roll of Honour contained the names of 376, out of a total membership of 800, and in addition to those who fell, 76 were wounded and 14 taken prisoners of war. The Old Kirk congregation has a remarkable record, being one of the oldest and most historic in Edinburgh.

TUESDAY 7th NOVEMBER 1939

Edinburgh City Police were today taking steps to secure more strict observance of the lighting restrictions. Shopkeepers in particular had been showing a certain laxity in obscuring their window and door lights in the early evening. It had been observed that blinds were not drawn until the last possible moment. Instructions had been issued to give the matter particular attention and a warning was given that any person found contravening the regulations would be dealt with by the authorities.

MONDAY 8th NOVEMBER 1736

The first-ever regular public theatre in Scotland opened in Carrubber's Close, Edinburgh.

SUNDAY 8th NOVEMBER 2009

Irish folk legends The Wolfe Tones played their first gig in Edinburgh for nearly 20 years, at the city's trendy Cabaret Voltaire venue in Blair Street. There were no arrests or trouble as 250 fans enjoyed a rare evening of ballads from their idols.

THURSDAY 9th NOVEMBER 1809

The future historian, essayist and social critic, Thomas Carlyle, arrived in Edinburgh during the afternoon and enrolled at Edinburgh University, aged just 15.

TUESDAY 9th NOVEMBER 1847

In Edinburgh, Sir James Young Simpson delivered Wilhelmina Carstairs while chloroform was administered to the mother, the first child to be born with the aid of modern anesthesia.

TUESDAY 10th NOVEMBER 1914

An appeal was launched via *The Scotsman* newspaper for warm clothes for the Western Front – in aid of the hundreds of thousands of Indian troops serving the empire there. The troops from the sub-continent had particular need for hats, gloves and, above all, cardigans, as they were simply not used to Europe's cold miserable November weather.

TUESDAY 10th NOVEMBER 1942

Another case of smallpox was admitted to Edinburgh City Hospital. The patient was from Berwickshire, but the case was traceable to the Edinburgh medical institution where the original outbreak occurred. There were 12 cases in hospital in the morning, but in the afternoon one died – an Edinburgh boy of 13 years of age who was one of the two first cases treated. There were, therefore, still 12 patients under treatment in the City Hospital. The number of suspected cases the day before increased from three to six, there being one more from Edinburgh and two from West Lothian, all of which were connected with the original outbreak.

FRIDAY 11th NOVEMBER 1938

The Norwegian football team, who were defeated by England at Newcastle during the week, visited Edinburgh. They were met by officials of the Hibernian and Heart of Midlothian football clubs and laid a wreath on the Stone of Remembrance. Later, the majority of the players took in some sightseeing in a search for Tommy Walker, the Hearts and Scotland inside-right, whom they had met earlier in their trip. The Norwegian team were not expected to play any further matches during their visit to the United Kingdom.

FRIDAY 12th NOVEMBER 1869

Edinburgh University became the first in Britain to allow women to study medicine – though not to graduate – but a woman, masquerading as Dr James Barry, had actually taken a medical degree at Edinburgh University in 1812 and became an army surgeon.

TUESDAY 12th NOVEMBER 1918

News reached the people of Edinburgh at around 11am that an armistice had been signed the day before and, thus, the Great War was finally over. Victory celebrations were quickly organised, special editions of newspapers were printed and many different types of flags – large and small – could be seen hanging from windows. The city was, for a time, immersed in jubilant sound, as horns were sounded and the Royal Navy squadron in The Forth sounded its sirens, making sure that anyone who was ignorant of the conflict's end would no longer be so.

MONDAY 13th NOVEMBER 1559

A huge force of Scottish 'Reformer' troops launched a disastrous assault on Mary of Guise's fort in Leith, which was easily repulsed by its Scottish and French defenders. The besiegers turned tail and fled all the way to Stirling.

WEDNESDAY 13th NOVEMBER 1850

Novelist Robert Louis Stevenson, best known for classic works such as *Treasure Island, Dr Jekyll and Mr Hyde* and *Kidnapped* was born in Edinburgh.

TUESDAY 14th NOVEMBER 1950

The 19-year-old Gunner, Derek Moore of the 69th Heavy Anti-Aircraft Regiment, was sentenced to 56 days' detention at a district court-martial at Redford Barracks, Edinburgh, when he was found guilty of being absent without leave. Moore, who was away from his unit at Redford from September 26th until his apprehension by the civil police at Dunstable on October 23rd, said that when he arrived at Sheffield on his way back from leave in Chesterfield, he had some time to wait for a train. He went to sleep in a carriage standing at a siding, and did not wake until over three hours after his train had departed.

THURSDAY 14th NOVEMBER 1968

Hibs boss Bob Shankly unleashed new signing Joe McBride on Hibs' opponents Lokomotiv Leipzig in the Fairs Cup second round first leg at Easter Road. McBride responded by netting Hibs' first hat-trick in European competition, and he should have had four but his second-half strike was ruled out by the Swiss referee, who was subsequently hit by a can of beer thrown by a disgusted fan. The first leg finished 3-1 to Hibs and the Hibees went on to win the second in East Germany 1-0.

MONDAY 15th NOVEMBER 1854

The famous 'Great fire of Edinburgh' broke out and lasted until 17th November. Among the places it destroyed were the High Street, Parliament Square and the Tron Kirk.

SATURDAY 15th NOVEMBER 1873

One of Edinburgh's most famous characters was immortalised in stone, when a statue of the dog Greyfriars Bobby – who stayed by his master's grave for 14 years – was unveiled. The Skye Terrier's owner was John Gray, who worked for the police as a night watchman.

MONDAY 16th NOVEMBER 1942

Edinburgh's smallpox epidemic continued as another death from the disease in the city – the second, and the fourth in all since the outbreak occurred – was reported. The latest victim was a man from Midlothian, aged 39, while the previous death in the hospital was a 13-year-old boy. The other two deaths, also traceable to one source in the Edinburgh area, occurred in Tranent and Lanarkshire. The position in Edinburgh therefore was summarised as follows: 'Seventeen proved cases of smallpox under treatment and four others under observation. There were six persons under observation on Sunday but since then two of these have been discharged from the City Hospital as free from infection.'

FRIDAY 16th NOVEMBER 1956

Driver James Kay, and conductor Andrew Birrell, made the last electric tram journey in the capital, taking the no.23 on a ceremonial trip to Shrubhill following a procession of trams from Braid Hills terminus to Morningside, watched by thousands.

FRIDAY 17th NOVEMBER 1961

Work began on stringing the main support cables across the Forth Road Bridge, a process expected to take some ten months using enough steel cable to stretch all the way around the Equator.

THURSDAY 18th NOVEMBER 1926

Edinburgh Dean of Guild Court granted an application by the Queen Mary Nursing Home to convert a self-contained house at 35 Chalmers Street into a maternity home and to build three bedrooms for nurses behind it. The cost of the scheme would be about £1,800.

WEDNESDAY 18th NOVEMBER 1936

Under the auspices of the King's Bodyguard for Scotland, The Royal Company of Archers, shooting for the Papirigo Medal took place at the Archery Butts, the Meadows, the winner being Mr Edward Boyd. Several other entrants complained about high winds making their shots go astray, but not Mr Boyd.

MONDAY 19th NOVEMBER 1934

A 22-year-old Edinburgh motorcyclist, John Barbour of 21, Bryson Road, died in the Royal Infirmary from injuries received on Saturday night following a collision between his machine and a woman pedestrian. The woman, Mrs Sarah McGlory, of 72 Montrose Terrace, Edinburgh, had to be detained in the infirmary, suffering from concussion.

SATURDAY 19th NOVEMBER 1994

Scotland's rugby union team played their first international at the newly completed, seated, covered and floodlit Murrayfield Stadium in front of 65,000 fans. Alas, the re-opening of the ground after substantial redevelopment was all the home fans had to cheer about, as Scotland lost to South Africa 10-34.

MONDAY 20th NOVEMBER 1911

A meeting of the District Committee decided roads in Edinburgh and the Lothians should be gritted both in summer and winter. JM Dudgeon blamed the tarmac roads for a rise in complaints about the surfaces, which he claimed have never really been suitable for horse traffic.

THURSDAY 20th NOVEMBER 2003

A £24 million Adventure Centre in Ratho, near Edinburgh, opened. The five-storey centre, which had taken almost ten years to come to fruition, was located in a quarry near the village and features the world's largest indoor climbing arena as well as an aerial assault course, mountain bike trails, and conference facilities. It had been expected to open the previous year but had been subject to a number of delays, one of which saw its Millennium Dome-style roof being ripped off in a violent storm that April. Despite concerns from city officials, the facility would be run by a private company rather than by the city's leisure authorities.

MONDAY 21st NOVEMBER 1938

Drama unfolded up Arthur's Seat as a young American geological student attending Edinburgh University was stranded for over an hour on one of the steepest cliff faces in King's Park. The climber got into difficulty when about three-quarters of the way up the face of the Eagle Rock, the landmark which lies between Samson's Ribs and the Gutted Haddie. When only a short distance from the summit he found himself confronted with a wall-like face of rock, and found he could neither advance nor retreat. A fellow student who accompanied him was powerless to assist his friend. Luckily, some boys were playing within hailing distance. He attracted their attention, and one of them rushed off to one of the lodges. On the way he met two of the park rangers, and informed them of the incident. The rangers succeeded in reaching a point higher up than where the student was stranded, and, helped by some of the public who had gathered by this time, they lowered a rope over the edge of the rock face and pulled the terrified American climber to safety.

SUNDAY 22nd NOVEMBER 1931

A 57-year-old woman named Catherine Storey or McFarlane, of 6 Society Buildings in Edinburgh, sadly died in Edinburgh Royal Infirmary as the result of a freak tramcar accident. She was descending the stairs of a tramcar in Granton when she fell and was catapulted onto the concrete platform at the roadside. Once again, the trams proved to be Edinburgh's most dangerous mode of transport.

MONDAY 22nd NOVEMBER 1971

Six Edinburgh schoolchildren who had gone missing while hillwalking in the Cairngorms were found dead by an RAF search and rescue team. A seventh child was still alive but rescuers were having great difficulty in getting him out, due to appalling weather conditions.

FRIDAY 23rd NOVEMBER 1928

Plans for a Memorial Hall at Colinton House, in memory of the former pupils of Merchiston Castle School who lost their lives in the Great War, were approved at Edinburgh Dean of Guild Court. The cost of the hall, which was to be erected so as to join two existing buildings, was estimated at £4,000. It was to be built of brick with stone facings and an open timbered roof, with accommodation for over 600 people.

THURSDAY 24th NOVEMBER 1440

The powerful 16-year-old William, Earl of Douglas, and his younger brother were invited to dine with the ten-year-old King James II's Chancellor and the ruling Regent, Sir Alexander Livingstone at Edinburgh Castle. They were quickly overpowered at 'The Black Dinner', then dragged outside and beheaded, at the behest of Livingstone.

SUNDAY 24th NOVEMBER 1861

Two 100-year-old tenement buildings collapsed on Edinburgh's Royal Mile, killing 35 people. Rescuers were sceptical about the chances of finding anyone alive amid the rubble until they heard the voice of one such survivor shouting; "Heave awa lads, am no deid yet." The man was rescued.

SUNDAY 25th NOVEMBER 1945

Three Edinburgh boys lost their lives, and one was seriously injured, as a result of a mortar bomb explosion which occurred at about half-past three in the afternoon in a wood near Kirkton Farm, Milton Bridge. Two of the three boys were killed instantaneously; the third perished from his injuries when he was being conveyed to Edinburgh Royal Infirmary in an ambulance. The three boys had gone for a walk at the Pentlands where they found an abandoned army mortar, which they set up and tested, sadly, to lethal effect.

THURSDAY 26th NOVEMBER 1914

Amid great euphoria, the entire Heart of Midlothian football team enlisted in the British Army en masse. They would undergo training at Hibernian's Easter Road ground, which had been turned over to the military. Their battalion later suffered appalling casualties on the Western Front.

TUESDAY 27th NOVEMBER 1923

The annual dog show and bazaar, in aid of the Scottish Society for the Prevention of Vivisection, was held in St Cuthbert's Hall in King's Stables Road. The 20 stalls, which were opened by a local Liberal parliamentary candidate, were laden with ornamental goods. In total, nearly £1,000 was raised, and the 'Top Dog' prize went to a Scottish Terrier.

SUNDAY 28th NOVEMBER 1666

The Battle of Rullion Green was fought on the Pentland Hills, south-west of Edinburgh, in which the King's army led by Sir Tam Dalyell easily defeated the Covenanters.

WEDNESDAY 29th NOVEMBER 1950

Edinburgh Corporation, like other Scottish local authorities, had been asked by the National Covenant Committee to pass a resolution in support of taking a plebiscite on a national basis on the question of reinstating or recreating a Scottish Parliament. But, the Lord Provost's Committee decided for 'no action', citing any such scheme's financial unsoundness as the reason.

SATURDAY 30th NOVEMBER 1996

A crowd consisting mostly of tourists and bussed-in schoolchildren turned out on the Royal Mile to see Prince Andrew lead a ceremonial procession to the castle bearing the ancient Stone of Destiny, which was being returned to Scotland after 700 years in English possession, having being removed from Scotland by Edward I during a failed attempt to conquer Scotland in 1296. The event was largely shunned by Edinburgh's populace – partly because many believed the stone to be a replica and also because it was being housed in Edinburgh rather than its original location of Scone, Perthshire. Nevertheless, there was much pomp and ceremony, including speeches and two artillery salutes.

DECEMBER

THURSDAY 1st DECEMBER 1768

The first-ever volume of *Encyclopedia Britannica* was published in Edinburgh, edited by Mr William Smellie.

THURSDAY 1st DECEMBER 1938

A movement was initiated to bring the 1946 Empire Games to Edinburgh. The proposal to host the prestigious games was bound up with the Sighthill sports ground scheme, which was to be discussed by the Parks Sub-Committee on the following Tuesday.

WEDNESDAY 2nd DECEMBER 1925

Three men appeared in the Burgh Court, Edinburgh, charged with attempting to sell cocaine. The men, all construction workers, tried to sell their illegal wares to a number of shopkeepers in Rose Street. Such was the potency of the substance seized from the men that Fergus Harris stated he had no option but to treat the matter gravely, even though it was the first recorded offence of its kind in Edinburgh. The men were given the option of a £3 fine or a term of imprisonment.

FRIDAY 2nd DECEMBER 1949

A jury sitting with Lord Guthrie in the Court of Session made an award of £4,000 compensation to Isabella Mackay from Gilmerton, who was currently still in hospital and had been declared insane after a steady decline in her physical and mental well-being since April 1948, when she was hit and almost killed by a falling chimney in Earl Grey Street.

SUNDAY 3rd DECEMBER 1944

All civilian defence and Home Guard units in Edinburgh were stood down or disbanded, with the threat of invasion by Nazi Germany now completely non-existent. Sir Andrew Thorne, G.O.C Scotland, took the final salute from the part-time soldiers on the steps outside the Royal Gallery in Princess Street.

THURSDAY 3rd DECEMBER 1998

Firefighters in the city battled for four hours to subdue a blaze at St Philip's Church in Joppa. The fire, which was thought to have been caused by a workman's blowtorch, destroyed the church roof and all of the internal fixtures and fittings.

TUESDAY 4th DECEMBER 1827

Two night watchmen at Liberton cemetery surprised each other while on separate patrols of the graveyard in an effort to keep out body-snatchers. Watchman Andrew Ewart opened fire on an intruder, killing him instantly, only to discover that he had killed his colleague Henry Penicuik, who had come to see why Ewart was taking so long.

SUNDAY 4th DECEMBER 1921

Residents of nearby Kirkliston had their Sunday-evening peace shattered at around 7pm by an almighty explosion. The noise was caused when civil explosive charges used for mining shale nearby were somehow detonated. Locals later likened the sound to that of an army ammunition dump being blown up. Though no-one was hurt, its cause was never established. Police were investigating the incident.

FRIDAY 5th DECEMBER 1930

A dog named 'Hearts Delight' was the star of the show at Powderhall Stadium, but was the bookies' nightmare as the dog's name, and recent form, meant it benefited greatly from 'sentimental betting'. Over 7,500 spectators packed the stadium and thoroughly enjoyed the meeting, despite much of the track being cloaked by thick fog, obscuring their view of some of the races. Extra race marshalls were employed to ensure the unexpected cloak of mist did not interfere with races.

TUESDAY 6th DECEMBER 1927

The United Free Presbytery of Edinburgh launched a verbal attack on the rise of gambling and other un-Christian-like behaviour in the capital. Their main target was the greyhound racing and its bookmakers, whom they derided as 'miniature racehorses' and 'godless rogues', respectively. One irate member of the Presbytery claimed gambling in Edinburgh was 'spreading like a prairie fire'.

FRIDAY 6th DECEMBER 1935

After many rumours and counter-rumours, which coupled the name of Alec Massie with in turn, Tottenham Hotspur, Brentford, Chelsea, and Aston Villa, the Heart of Midlothian international right half-back was transferred to Aston Villa, at a fee reported to be £6,400, which, if it was correct, was the highest transfer figure ever paid for a Hearts player.

MONDAY 7th DECEMBER 1914

Sir George McCrae's newly raised battalion of volunteers, comprised mostly of men from Lothian, reached the impressive numerical strength of 1,350, with 115 men enlisting today alone. The battalion is of the 'pals' type endorsed by Lord Kitchener of Omdurman in his incessant recruitment drive, and though the recruits may lack experience, their zeal for king and country has impressed observers from The War Office, who have sanctioned the battalion's establishment. A number of Hearts players were in its ranks.

THURSDAY 7th DECEMBER 1933

Detective William Merrilees was not in court to witness the culmination of what his police work had been partly responsible for. Asher Barnard, proprietor of the Kosmo Dance Club, however, was in Edinburgh Sheriff Court, found guilty of offences under the Immoral Traffic Act and the Criminal Law Amendment Act, and was sentenced to 18 months' imprisonment. Edwin Jones, described as manager, and James Black, floor manager in the same club, were found guilty by the jury of aiding and abetting in prostitution, and were each sentenced to three months' imprisonment.

TUESDAY 8th DECEMBER 1936

A young man who threw a sauce bottle at a mirror in an Edinburgh fish restaurant was sent to prison for 20 days by Gilzean at Edinburgh Court. The man, William Boyd of 306 Lawnmarket, admitted having conducted himself in a disorderly manner, committing a breach of the peace, and maliciously breaking the mirror.

SUNDAY 8th DECEMBER 2002

Part of Edinburgh's Old Town has been left in ruins by a fire that razed historic buildings and forced 150 people to flee their homes. Firefighters battled throughout the day to bring under control a blaze that started shortly after 8pm on Saturday night. The blaze raged through the Cowgate area of the city, part of a UNESCO world heritage site, and at one point threatened some of the city's most significant buildings. The cost was being estimated at millions of pounds. However, after more than 80 firefighters doused the area with water, Edinburgh's most architecturally significant buildings, like the nearby Adam House, were spared.

WEDNESDAY 9th DECEMBER 1947

The Drill Hall in Grindlay Street, Edinburgh, began hosting an exhibition that would give shoppers an insight into how they will buy things in future years. A new 'self-service' checkout, of the type often seen in North America, was on display and was wowing shoppers – both housewives and nosey shopkeepers alike. It was claimed the new system cuts costs for retailers and speeds up shopping for consumers. Though those who had seen the system work had been impressed, some had expressed concern that this new type of technology may keep people out of jobs.

SATURDAY 9th DECEMBER 1972

A battling performance from Hibs at Hampden Park saw the Hibees win the League Cup Final against Jock Stein's formidable Celtic team. Pat Stanton and Jimmy O'Rourke netted for Hibs, with young Kenny Dalglish scoring Celtic's consolation. Edinburgh welcomed its heroes back with an open-top bus parade. Hibs' boss Eddie Turnbull was as dignified in victory as his counterpart Stein was gracious in defeat. Hibs would not win another major trophy until the 1991 League Cup victory.

TUESDAY 10th DECEMBER 1930

An eight-year-old schoolgirl, Roseanne McCrae of Leith, was knocked down by a Corporation bus at the junction of Henderson Street and Great Junction Street in Leith. The accident occurred shortly after six o'clock. The girl, who had a dog with her, apparently ran in front of the bus, and was struck by one of its wheels. She was taken to Leith Hospital, but died about an hour later.

SUNDAY 11th DECEMBER 1949

An unusually interesting event took place in Edinburgh when a full-length film from the Soviet Union was given its British premiere. The picture was 'Ballerina', and it was shown by Edinburgh Film Guild in the Caley Picture House. The film was of the greatest interest to audiences in this country because it gave them an opportunity to see one of the foremost ballerinas of their day, Galina Ulanova, dancing in a Russian performance of 'The Swan Lake'.

MONDAY 12th DECEMBER 1932

Alexander Mann, a 21-year-old slater, was fined £5 with the alternative of 30 days in prison at Edinburgh Sheriff Court. He pleaded guilty to three charges of stealing rose bushes and a charge of stealing a motor car. It was stated that the accused stole the bushes from gardens in Stenhouse Avenue. The motor car had been left in the street and the accused had pushed it about 50 yards. He was found trying to start it, although he could not even drive a motor vehicle. Mr Mann claimed that he had stolen the rose bushes with the intent of giving them to his estranged sweetheart.

TUESDAY 12th DECEMBER 1950

It was reported at a meeting of Edinburgh Trades Council that a 'serious instance of unemployment' existed among bricklayers in the Edinburgh area, the reason being given as a chronic shortage of bricks. Negotiations were to take place with the Secretary of State for Scotland to obtain an increased supply of bricks for the area.

SUNDAY 13th DECEMBER 1942

Jews throughout Britain observed a day of fasting and mourning for the one-and-a-half million Jews who had been massacred in Poland by the Nazis. At a special memorial service held in the Synagogue at Salisbury Road, Edinburgh, a great crowd of people attending included a considerable number of Gentile sympathisers and friends, as well as MPs, local dignitaries and several high-ranking officers of Allied armies in exile. This was the second instance of Edinburgh showing support for the Jews in recent years, following the savage attacks on Mosley's Blackshirts in the 1930s.

WEDNESDAY 13th DECEMBER 1950

A Christmas tree presented to Edinburgh by Copenhagen was erected at the Mound without any mishap, unlike the previous year, when the tree broke. Last night men worked, by aid of floodlights, on the tubular scaffolding erected round the tree to enable the coloured light bulbs to be put on. The tree rose to an impressive height, and seven scaffolding stages were necessary to allow men to work from ground level to its top.

TUESDAY 14th DECEMBER 1976

A solution to the dispute between pub managers and Scottish Breweries was expected to be announced after managers agreed a pay deal for working longer hours, closing at 11pm, rather than at 10pm as before. A brewery spokesman had expressed delight at the news and also at how bar staff coped with the new longer opening hours. Lothian and Borders police stated that there had been a relaxed and orderly atmosphere in Edinburgh's pubs, both during drinking hours and during dispersal at closing time.

THURSDAY 14th DECEMBER 1989

The final link in Edinburgh's 14-mile dual carriageway bypass road, built around the southern perimeter over the last ten years at a cost of £72m, was opened officially by Lothian Region Convener James Cook. This fifth section, completed eight months ahead of schedule by Miller Construction, runs 2.8 miles from the A701 at Straiton Road to the A68 at Sheriffhall, giving a direct flow between the A8 at Gogarburn in the west, and the A1 at Newcraighall in the east. Miller Group civil engineering director John Carson said it would transform communications between central and east Scotland and ease congestion in Edinburgh.

THURSDAY 15th DECEMBER 1927

While playing football in McDonald Road this afternoon, Thomas McKinnon, aged six, from Spey Street, was knocked down by a motor car. He sustained serious head injuries, a compound fracture of the left leg, and his right arm was broken. He was removed to the Royal Infirmary, where he lay in a serious condition. Doctors feared they may have to amputate his leg.

TUESDAY 15th DECEMBER 1936

A young man who appeared before Sheriff-Principal Brown at Edinburgh Sheriff Court was sent to borstal for three years. He was James John McCurdy, aged just 19, and he admitted having assaulted William George Lamb, a bank agent, in the common stair leading to his house at 48 Spottiswoode Road, Edinburgh. The charge bore that he struck Lamb repeatedly on the head and face with a piece of rubber tubing loaded with lead, or other instrument, and that he kicked him on the head and body, with intent to rob him.

MONDAY 16th DECEMBER 1661

Many of Scotland's important historical records were lost when the ship *Elizabeth of Burntisland* sank off the English coast. The records had been taken to London by Oliver Cromwell and were being returned home to Edinburgh.

TUESDAY 16th DECEMBER 1924

A labourer was killed in a horrific accident at a grain miller's premises in Bath Street, Leith. The 33-year-old George Jeffrey, himself a Leith man, overbalanced and fell down the well of a hoist, falling some 20 feet.

FRIDAY 17th DECEMBER 1920

The question of spending the £44,000 grant of the Ministry of Transport in providing work which would reduce the number of unemployed in the city was under consideration at a meeting of the Streets and Buildings Committee of Edinburgh Town Council. The Council at their last meeting had decided that work should be commenced at once on the widening of the Peffermill Road and on the making of a new road from Firhill (Redford) to Comiston Road.

SUNDAY 17th DECEMBER 1939

Blinders, a black cocker spaniel, collected £3 15s in Edinburgh for the Red Cross Fund. He wore a red saddle with a box at each side and when the boxes became too heavy for comfort he cast appealing glances at his mistress to have them emptied and to let him start afresh. One man, who confessed to having already given £100 to the Red Cross, said he could not resist the appeal of the spaniel's lovely eyes.

SATURDAY 18th DECEMBER 1943

Captain Douglas Ford of Edinburgh, an officer in the Royal Scots 2nd Battalion which was forced to surrender on Christmas Day 1941 in Hong Kong, was executed by firing squad after his Japanese captors had found him guilty of being a spy after he had managed to make contact with Allied intelligence, despite being held in a Japanese POW camp. Ford never revealed who his co-conspirators in the camp were, and received a posthumous George Cross in recognition of 'his conspicuous gallantry'.

THURSDAY 18th DECEMBER 2003

In a rearranged televised League Cup quarter-final, just under 10,000 fans at Easter Road saw Hibs defeat Celtic to progress to the semi-finals of the competition for the second time in three seasons. Stan Varga gave Celtic the lead but the Hibees, who for once played a physical style of football, equalised through a Grant Brebner penalty before a late strike by youngster Kevin Thomson sealed the win for Bobby Williamson's men.

MONDAY 19th DECEMBER 1904

The Scotsman newspaper opened its brand new offices and printing works on Edinburgh's trendy North Bridge.

TUESDAY 19th DECEMBER 1950

Sentences of three months' imprisonment each were imposed at Edinburgh Sheriff Court on George Attchison and his wife, Ellen Fraser or Attchison, both of 3 Boothacre Cottages in Leith. They were found guilty, after trial, of having wilfully neglected their seven children, whose ages ranged from one to 10 years. Inspectors of the Leith SSPCC stated the children were dirty and poorly clothed. The house was in a shocking condition, and there was insufficient bedding.

FRIDAY 20th DECEMBER 1935

The frost continued to hold Scotland in its grip, while England is not only frost-bound but fog-bound. The roads were in a dangerous condition in many areas. Owing to the fog, trains from England were late in reaching Edinburgh. Thanks to her bicycle skidding on the icy roadway, Muriel Brown, aged 16, of 12 Mountcastle Crescent, Edinburgh, lay in Edinburgh Royal Infirmary suffering from concussion. She was found unconscious, beside her bicycle, in Northfield Road.

WEDNESDAY 20th DECEMBER 1950

The Mary Erskine School for Girls held their Christmas Carol Service in Chalmers Church, West Port this afternoon. Before a large congregation, consisting of parents and friends, the school choir, although rather cramped for space, gave excellent renderings of several carols. Outstanding amongst these were Benjamin Britten's ceremony of carols, *There Is No Rose* and Vaughan Williams' arrangement of the Sussex traditional air *On Christmas Night All Christians Sing*.

FRIDAY 21st DECEMBER 1917

An example of the efficiency of the communal feeding kitchens under the Edinburgh Food Control Committee, and their ability to cope with an emergency, was provided today. At two o'clock in the afternoon, though there was no material at the cooking centre, they undertook to provide a three-course dinner for a party of 450 soldiers arriving at 6pm. It was successfully accomplished.

SUNDAY 21st DECEMBER 1930

When fire broke out in a dwelling house at 5 Inglis Green Road, Slateford, Edinburgh, an occupant of the house, Mrs Woodrow, aged 70, had to be removed to a neighbour's house as the result of shock. She was otherwise uninjured. The Edinburgh Brigade subdued the outbreak after part of the kitchen and furnishings had been destroyed.

MONDAY 22nd DECEMBER 1924

Considerable alarm was caused early in the morning in the neighbourhood of Clerk Street, Edinburgh, by a boiler explosion in the premises of J McCarthy, the baker in Clerk Street. A heavy iron door was broken in two and a large plate-glass window in the front of the shop was blown into the street. An employee on duty at the time was slightly injured and suffered from shock, but after receiving attention at Edinburgh Royal Infirmary he was allowed to proceed to his home. The explosion was said to have been caused by an accumulation of gas from coal in the boiler fire.

WEDNESDAY 22nd DECEMBER 1925

For having left a car abandoned in Princes Street on November 25th for two hours, a period longer than was necessary for the taking up or setting down of passengers, Frederick J Hood of 9 Bellevue Terrace in Edinburgh was fined £1 at Edinburgh Burgh Court.

WEDNESDAY 23rd DECEMBER 1931

An old man, James McQuain of 53 Easter Road, fell into the water whilst drunk at the south side of the Edinburgh Dock in Leith. He was rescued by two employees of the Dock Commission who were in the vicinity at the time of the accident.

TUESDAY 23rd DECEMBER 1947

A girl of five and a woman of 67 were victims of fatal accidents in Edinburgh. Mrs Margaret Senior or Knight, aged 61 from 49 Peffermill Road, was killed when she was struck by a lorry while crossing Peffermill Road at 5pm. Katherine Donaldson Grantham Shillinglaw, the five-year-old from 21 Niddrie Mains Terrace, was struck by a lorry when she ran from the pavement in Niddrie Mains Road, and sustained injuries from which she died before reaching Edinburgh Royal Infirmary. In both instances, black ice on roads has been cited as the main cause of these tragic accidents.

TUESDAY 24th DECEMBER 1650

Having heroically defended Edinburgh Castle from Cromwell's siege for three months following the Scots' defeat at Dunbar, the Earl of Dundas was finally compelled to surrender the fortress to the English, as he had no hope of being relieved in the near future. Cromwell hanged Dundas' deputy after the siege ended, contrary to promises he had earlier made to the beleaguered garrison, later claiming he had taken such action in retaliation for an earlier sniping incident.

TUESDAY 24th DECEMBER 2002

A nationwide police operation against suspected terrorists culminated in the arrest and detention of four Arab men in and around the Leith area in connection with a conspiracy to cause explosions. The four accused were all remanded to Kilmarnock Prison in Ayrshire.

FRIDAY 25th DECEMBER 2009

A few crisp, white flakes of snow were confirmed as having fallen on Edinburgh Castle, giving Scotland's capital city its first white Christmas in five years. Disgruntled bookmakers, who thought that a brief thaw had eradicated any such possibility, had to pay out at 3/1. Most of Scotland also had a white Christmas, at least technically.

SATURDAY 25th DECEMBER 2010

Local restaurant owner and Muslim Assader Ali brought some Christmas cheer to Edinburgh's homeless people by giving out hundreds of free Turkey Jalfrezi meals, using his fleet of four delivery vehicles.

MONDAY 26th DECEMBER 1932

A draw was the result of a well-contested game at Raeburn Place between the Edinburgh Academicals and the London Scottish in the annual Christmas engagement. Both clubs were well represented, and the match attracted about 5,000 spectators. The Academicals were the better side in the early half and were well worthy of their one-try lead at the interval, though it took them a long time to secure it, which was scored by G E Potts. The final score was 3-3.

THURSDAY 26th DECEMBER 2006

A rare Boxing Day encounter saw Hearts take on Hibs at Tynecastle, with the Jambos thirsting for revenge after the Easter Road side had knocked them out of the cup a few weeks previously. Hearts turned on the style and went 2-0 up, thanks to direct play and some goalkeeping buffoonery by Hibs custodian Zibi Malkowski. Hibs fought back and levelled the match at 2-2 but had Dean Shiels sent off after some unsportsmanlike play-acting by Hearts' Craig Gordon after Shiels had beaten him from the spot. The thrilling match ended 3-2 to Hearts, Jankauskas, Mikoliunas and Hartley scoring for the home side while Shiels (pen) and Chris Killen netted for Hibs.

THURSDAY 27th DECEMBER 1928

Sir George McCrae, the publicist and man who famously roused up large crowds of Edinburgh men into joining his 'pals' battalion for service in the Great War, died aged 69 after a long illness. He fought in the British defeat at the Somme in 1916 and, when not soldiering, was also a Justice of the Peace in Edinburgh.

MONDAY 27th DECEMBER 1993

Just over 10,000 fans made it to a freezing Easter Road to see Hibernian turn on the style and thrash Partick Thistle 5-1. Hibs' scorers were Hamilton, Wright, Jackson, McAllister and David Farrell, who scored his first goal for the club with a long-range effort. Grant Tierney's stunning second-half overhead kick goal was of scant consolation to the Jags. Hibs' David Farrell was later chased by boss Alex Miller when he asked for the match ball in recognition of his rare goal, a privilege usually the sole preserve of hat-trick scorers.

FRIDAY 28th DECEMBER 1934

Many widows of Royal Scots killed in action during the war renewed their association with the regiment in Edinburgh. In company with widows and children of men of the regiment who had died since the war, they assembled in the Drill Hall in East Claremont Street, Edinburgh, the occasion being the annual entertainment organised by the Royal Scots Club. Altogether, 700 guests sat down to tea in the gaily decorated hall – 400 widows and 300 children. Lord Henry Scott, chairman of the club, announced he had received a message from the Princess Royal, Colonel-in-Chief of the regiment, in which she expressed the hope that all present would thoroughly enjoy themselves.

WEDNESDAY 28th DECEMBER 1949

Edinburgh police were anxious to trace a man who alighted from a Corstorphine-bound tramcar at Balgreen Road, at 9.20pm, along with a man and woman. A private motor car travelling westwards collided with the man and woman, resulting in the woman being fatally injured and her male companion slightly injured. Police had stressed they only wished to interview the man, not arrest him, and had urged him to come forward.

SUNDAY 29th DECEMBER 1918

Named after the French commander of Quebec in 1757, the flagship *Montcalm* left the Firth of Forth in the company of her three destroyers, heading for Cherbourg. The day before, the French sailors bid Edinburgh goodbye and were conspicuous by their smart uniforms and their singing of 'Le Marseillaise' as they walked the streets of the capital, where they had been warmly received by local men and women alike. The ships would then depart for Oran in North Africa.

WEDNESDAY 29th DECEMBER 1948

Used as a government storage facility since the outbreak of war in 1939, Edinburgh's Murrayfield Ice Rink now looked set to be given back to its original purpose. A Ministry of Works official today confirmed that a new store was being built at Sighthill, meaning that the £55,000 rink could be freed up in little more than a year.

MONDAY 30th DECEMBER 1939

In the beautifully decorated Winter Garden of Leith Hospital, about 300 children attending the outpatient department of the hospital were entertained to tea and a concert. The entertainment, which was much appreciated by the children, was provided by Mrs Corsar-Rosely-Arbroath, who has done much to cheer up the little patients of the institution. After the concert today the children received fruit and sweets. Three thousand poor children also spent a happy time at the Capitol, Leith, where they were entertained to a splendid programme of pictures. They greatly enjoyed the fare, and on leaving the building, were each presented with a bag of buns and fruit.

SATURDAY 30th DECEMBER 1995

Hibs travelled to Ibrox having already beaten the champions there earlier in the season, and looking for a morale-boosting result ahead of the coming New Year derby. They didn't get it. The Ibrox side humiliated Alex Miller's men 7-0, with ex-Hibs player Gordon Durie scoring four goals. Charlie Miller, Paul Gascoigne and Oleg Salenko completed the rout.

TUESDAY 31st DECEMBER 1811

Two people were killed and dozens more were injured when Hogmanay in Edinburgh exploded in an orgy of violence. Two large gangs of teenagers were responsible for the bedlam that ensued in the city as policemen were attacked, churches raided and ordinary citizens beaten up and robbed. The Tron Kirk was ransacked.

SUNDAY 31st DECEMBER 2006

Edinburgh's Hogmanay street party was cancelled for reasons relating to public health and safety amid utterly atrocious weather conditions. Events cancelled because of torrential rain and high winds included the Royal Bank Street Party, the Concert in the Gardens and the Ceilidh. However, less severe wind conditions in the few minutes before midnight allowed six of the Seven Hills' fireworks to be set-off, with a restricted firing of fireworks on the seventh hill, Castle Hill.

BIBLIOGRAPHY

The Edinburgh Encyclopedia – Sandy Mull
Bank of Scotland 1695-1995 – Alan Cameron
Edinburgh: A celebration – Michael Russell
Edinburgh – Allan Massie
Capital of the mind – James Buchan
Scotland: A history – Jenny Wormald

Encyclopedia of Scottish Battles – Chris Brown PhD
Tales of Edinburgh Castle – Stuart MacHardy MA
Archives, miscellaneous: *The Times, The Herald, The Scotsman, Edinburgh Evening News, The Daily Record* and the Edinburgh Room at the library on George IV Bridge.

The website iHibs